GLORY
VEILED AND
UNVEILED

"BUT WHEN HE WAS YET
   A GREAT WAY OFF..."

The Prodigal's Father
by Karl Kwekel

GLORY VEILED AND UNVEILED

A Heart-Searching Look at Christ's Parables

Gerald M. Bilkes

Reformation Heritage Books
Grand Rapids, Michigan

Reformation Heritage Books
2965 Leonard St. NE
Grand Rapids, MI 49525
616-977-0889 / Fax 616-285-3246
orders@heritagebooks.org
www.heritagebooks.org

Printed in the United States of America
12 13 14 15 16 17/10 9 8 7 6 5 4 3 2 1

Library of Congress Cataloging-in-Publication Data

Bilkes, Gerald M.
  Glory veiled and unveiled : a heart-searching look at Christ's parables / Gerald M. Bilkes.
       p. cm.
  ISBN 978-1-60178-165-9 (pbk. : alk. paper) 1. Jesus Christ—Parables. I. Title.
  BT375.3.B55 2012
  226.8'06—dc23
                                       2012000924

For additional Reformed literature, both new and used, request a free book list from Reformation Heritage Books at the above regular or e-mail address.

Contents

The Glory of Kingdom Grace:
Some Parables in Luke

The Glory of Kingdom Consummation:
More Parables from Matthew

The Glory of Christ the King:
The Parables of John

Conclusion

To Michelle,
with love

Acknowledgments

I am greatly indebted to Jay Collier, Annette Gysen, and the other staff at RHB for seeing this book through to publication, and for Dr. Joel Beeke for agreeing to publish it. Much of this book appeared in installments in the *Banner of Sovereign Grace Truth* and *The Messenger*, and I gratefully acknowledge the respective editors, Dr. Joel Beeke and Rev. Cornelis Pronk, for permission to publish them in this format. I wish to thank Karl Kwekel for generously allowing me to use his *The Prodigal's Father* for the front cover.

A special thanks to those who helped proofread parts or the whole: Michelle (my wife), Kate DeVries (sister-in-law), Pauline Timmer (mother-in-law), Ann Dykema, Dr. Lawrence Bilkes (my dad), and Rev. Lawrence J. Bilkes (my brother). I want to acknowledge students in PRTS seminary classes who often helped improve my understanding of individual parables. A special thank-you to Rev. Maarten Kuivenhoven and Dirk Naves, my research assistants in the past, and Michael Borg, currently assisting me, for their work toward this volume. Also, I have appreciated the encouragement from my colleagues at the seminary, Dr. Joel Beeke, Dr. David Murray, and Dr. William VanDoodewaard. I want to acknowledge the Free Reformed Churches, specifically the Theological Education Committee, for their help and encouragement, and especially for allowing me the privilege of a sabbatical semester (spring 2011), during which I was able to put the finishing touches on this book.

I thank my mom and dad for teaching me the value of the Scriptures from early days. Their parents also showed a love for the Scriptures and the Christ of the Scriptures, for which I am very thankful. Grandma Westerveld: I still remember the time you told me that Grandpa found himself in the publican, praying, "O God, wees mij zondaar genadig" (O God, be merciful to me a sinner). I am thankful for those preachers whom the Lord used to pursue me with the message of the parables in ways that the Lord blessed to my heart. Above all, I thank the Lord our gracious God for the privilege of discovering "treasure hid in a field" (Matt. 13:44).

Introduction

You have likely read the parables of Christ before, perhaps many times. But have *they* read *you?* This question will probably seem very strange at the outset. "How can passages read me?" you wonder. "Words on a page don't have eyes or a mind so that they can read me. Besides, I am not a book full of pages with words to be read."

Admittedly, we don't typically think or talk like this. Yet we miss something important as a result. Think of what happened when the prophet Nathan came to David the king with the parable of the young lamb (2 Sam. 12:1–6). It ended up revealing the sin in David's life that, until that point, he had been unable to see. Nathan's parable acted as a searchlight on David's heart and uncovered something that David had been concealing beneath layers of excuses and attempts to suppress his guilt. David grasped the parable that day. But, more importantly, the parable grasped him.

Without a doubt, it was the Holy Spirit who was working in David to produce accurate self-knowledge. But this parable was the means used to that end. It should be no surprise that the Spirit loves to use the Word. After all, He has inspired it (2 Peter 1:21). He is pleased to use it to bring sinners to a true and saving knowledge of God and themselves (John 16:8–14).

Yet many today are content to read the Bible in a way in which the Word of God is subject to them, rather than reading so *they* are subject to the Word. They study the Bible—so they think—but the Bible does not study them. They may even "search the Scriptures," but the Scriptures fail to search them.

Experimental Reading of the Bible

There are many books on the parables that are readily available. I did not simply wish to distill from their findings or duplicate their efforts. The concern of this book, rather, is to help students of Scripture read the parables in a way that takes into account that Scripture is searching us; we ought, then, to expect Scripture to transform us.

When we expect God to use His Word to search and change us, we take what theologians have called the "experimental" (or "experiential") approach to the Scriptures. In fact, when you come to Scripture truly believing it to be what it claims to be—the Word of God—and submitting to its scrutiny of all of your life, then you are reading the Word experimentally. Psalm 119 is one glorious expression of experimental reading, and verse 130 states it succinctly: "The entrance of thy words giveth light; it giveth understanding to the simple."

The problem is that by nature everything is out of order in our lives. We don't see things as they truly are. Sin has drawn a veil over our hearts, and we love this darkness rather than the light (John 3:19). By nature, we have lost the sense of being subject to God and accountable to Him. Actually, it is even worse than that. We actively rebel against His authority and transgress His laws (Rom. 8:7). We imagine we can make God submit to us. We make His Word the object of our scrutiny, rather than submitting ourselves to its scrutiny. Many Bible students and teachers think they understand the Bible, and yet they do not subject their lives to it. They "understand" the Bible like a band of rebels might understand the laws of a government against which they fight every day.

But thankfully, through the equipping work of the Holy Spirit in their lives, people throughout the centuries have learned to read and explain Scripture in a truly experimental way. Anyone who has read Augustine, Bernard of Clairvaux, John Calvin, John Bunyan, John Owen, Jonathan Edwards— just to name a few—will have had a taste of this. And yet, in recent years, universities, churches, and people everywhere have avoided and derided experimental reading. Truly, "the natural man receiveth not the things of the Spirit of God" (1 Cor. 2:14).[1]

Sometimes people will tell you that experimental interpretation of Scripture is something superimposed upon Scripture. They imagine it as an "extra" that comes from mystically inclined minds, those who are not content with the plain meaning of Scripture. Admittedly, a stream of interpreters throughout the centuries have done a lot to give credence to this charge. But the abuse of experimental interpretation doesn't mean it is not necessary or useful when done properly.

How This Book Is Organized
There are between thirty-five and sixty of Christ's parables recorded in Scripture, depending on how they are counted. I

---

1. For more on this, see my "Heart-Reading: Recovering a Spiritual Approach to Scripture," *Puritan Reformed Theological Journal* 1, no. 2 (2009): 12–22.

have selected about twenty-five of them. Those who are interested in further study will be able to apply the method used in this book to other parables.

At times, when several of the parables deal with one topic, I have grouped them together into one chapter. I have not set out to give each parable an exhaustive treatment. Instead, I aim to point out overarching themes and pursue avenues of application for each parable covered. I have formatted the chapters in such a way as to assist in personal or group Bible study. There are questions at the end of each chapter that aim to help the reader further digest the parable.

In the interest of demonstrating how the parables should be read experimentally, I have arranged each chapter according to four categories:

1. *The Scenery*: How does Christ use the context, setting, background, and culture reflected in the parable to reach within human hearts?

2. *The Substance*: What is the main message that Christ gives in the parable about His kingdom or aspects of it?

3. *The Savior*: What does the parable unveil about the glorious Savior, His person and His work, to those who believe?

4. *The Searchlight*: In what ways does the parable search our hearts and lives and expose what is in them, as well as guide us into the knowledge of Christ as the gracious and glorious king of the kingdom?

Approaching the Parables

Awakening to Glory

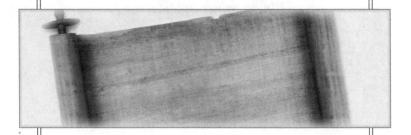

THE RADIANCE OF THE SCRIPTURES
(Isaiah 6:1–10)

In the year that king Uzziah died I saw also the
LORD sitting upon a throne, high and lifted up,
and his train filled the temple. Above it stood the
seraphims: each one had six wings; with twain he
covered his face, and with twain he covered his
feet, and with twain he did fly. And one cried unto
another, and said, Holy, holy, holy, is the LORD
of hosts: the whole earth is full of his glory. And
the posts of the door moved at the voice of him
that cried, and the house was filled with smoke.

—ISAIAH 6:1–4

1

Frequently, the Bible tells us of someone who, as it were, wakes up to the reality of the glory of the Lord. Isaiah certainly experienced this in the vision he records in Isaiah 6. The Lord allowed him to see within the throne room of heaven, and there he saw the majesty of the Lord (vv. 1–2). Christ later explained that what Isaiah saw on that occasion was His glory (John 12:41). On the one hand, this experience of the glory of the Lord left Isaiah feeling undone (v. 5). On the other hand, it mastered him to such an extent that he was willing to go and preach the coming kingdom of God (v. 8).

Earlier, Moses had a similar experience in the desert of Horeb (Ex. 3:1–2). While tending Jethro's sheep, he saw a great sight that proved to be life-altering for him—an appearance of the glory of the Lord. Moses saw a bush burning, but not burning up. In the end, God explained from the bush that He had come down to deliver His people. When Moses awoke to the reality of God speaking to him in glory, like Isaiah, he responded in absolute fear and dread. We read that he "hid his face; for he was afraid to look upon God" (Ex. 3:6).

You could say that both of these experiences were awakening experiences. Until then, these men had not known or seen the radiance and splendor of the glory of God. But when God's glory appeared to them, they were completely transformed. They felt their insignificance and sinfulness. But ultimately they were mastered by the glory of God to serve Him.

Once, Peter literally awoke to the glory of the Lord. He was with two other disciples who had come to a mountain in Galilee to pray. It was the occasion that we know as the transfiguration of Christ. For some reason, Peter and the others were asleep during the first part of this transfiguration. Then we read, "And when they were awake, they saw his glory" (Luke 9:32). Christ was there in glory, and His face and clothes shone as the disciples had never seen before. Moreover, they heard a voice from heaven, saying, "This is my beloved Son: hear him" (Luke 9:35). What an awakening that must have been!

God's Glorious Word

Many imagine that hearing a voice from heaven would be a wonderful experience. "That would be glorious," they think, "far surpassing anything we have in the Scriptures." But the apostle Peter, who was there, writes, "We have also a more sure word of prophecy" than a voice from heaven (2 Peter 1:19). By this "more sure word" he means the Scriptures. In other words, if you had given Peter the choice between a voice from heaven or the written Word of God, he would have decidedly chosen the latter. To him the Scriptures were eminently glorious.

The matter is really quite simple. Since the Word of God is what it professes to be—the Word of God—it comes with a glory second to none. Let's think for a moment together about what *glory* actually is. We sometimes speak of a glorious day, and by that we typically mean a day with a lot of sunshine. Because of the luster of the sunshine, we see the magnificence of everything more easily and readily than on a cloudy and dreary day.

This helps illustrate how the Bible understands glory. According to the Bible, glory is the splendor that flows from a person's authority. In Hebrew, the word we translate as *glory* literally means "weight." It is what you would feel if a king or other important person were in your presence. You would feel small in comparison with that person's importance, similar to how you might feel when you see the splendor of creation in the brilliant light of the sun. If we sense this feeling with some great person here on earth or in creation around us, how much more should we feel this with regard to God Himself, who has made all of creation and is greater than all.

Glory Veiled

One of the main reasons many who handle Scripture do not see its profound, sin-exposing, life-altering glory is they do not submit to it as God's Word. Somehow, in theory and practice, the Word of God has been reduced to merely human words. Thus the glory is gone, at least from the minds and experience of the readers. The Word of God seems common and ordinary, more human than divine. Our natural minds are blind to the weight of the glory of Scripture.

In order, then, to read the Scriptures experimentally, as they should be read, we need to recognize, register, and respond inwardly to the glory they possess as the Word of God. However, with the parables of Christ, we need to realize that something more is going on. In the parables, Christ is intentionally veiling or concealing His glory and the glory of His kingdom.

Many miss this point. They imagine Jesus spoke in parables simply to make His teaching easy, simple, and alluring for anyone who heard them. But if this was the case, why, then, did so many fail to appreciate the parables? Especially those in authority rejected their teaching (e.g., Matt. 21:45–46). Christ Himself explained what He was doing when He answered the disciples' question about why He chose to speak in parables. He states it this way: "Unto you it is given to know the mystery of the kingdom of God: but unto them that are without, all these things are done in parables: that seeing they may see, and not perceive; and hearing they may hear, and not understand; lest at any time they should be converted, and their sins should be forgiven them" (Mark 4:11–12). In other words, in the parables Christ is veiling His glory to conceal it from some, although He is ultimately revealing it to others.

The veiling of Christ's glory began already when He became incarnate of the Virgin Mary. Think of how He was conceived and born in relative obscurity. He grew up and reached adulthood, still hidden from the public eye. Not until He was thirty years old did He begin His public ministry. Truly, He was laying aside His glory in these things. Even as He began His work in public, He concealed His glory from the multitudes, though from time to time He would unveil something of it in His teaching and miracles.

In fact, even His disciples did not understand the full meaning of many things that Christ was teaching. It was as if the truths about which He spoke were hidden, or veiled. Proverbs 25:2 makes an interesting observation regarding this: "It is the glory of God to conceal a thing: but the honour of kings is to search out a matter." As the divine Son of God, it was Christ's prerogative to conceal. As strange as it sounds, Christ ultimately would prove Himself more glorious by first hiding that glory.

Let me give a simple example to which we can all relate. Think of how much more intriguing it is to receive a gift that is wrapped, even with simple paper, than to receive a gift without wrapping. The wrapping begs to be taken away so the gift can be seen. So too the parables "wrap" the glory of Christ. Those who are spiritually blind—and thus are without humble, teachable faith—are blind to this glory. They see only the plain "wrapping," and because there is no true faith, they never receive what is inside. They might find a certain measure of attraction in these simple stories, but the mysteries of the kingdom and the king of the kingdom are hid to them. Those who believe, on the other hand, are shown something of this king and kingdom.

The Ancient Tabernacle

Another helpful comparison is the ancient tabernacle, a special symbol of God's reign of grace among His people. His glory was certainly concealed there, as He sat enthroned between the cherubim. The tabernacle used many coverings and veils that hid items of glory and mystery. To many people it was only a little tent with a lot of curtains around it; it was not the hallmark of anything glorious or divine. Interestingly, the items in the tabernacle were quite ordinary and everyday kinds of things. We would say, colloquially speaking, there were a fireplace, a washbasin, a candlestick, a table with bread, a footstool, and a few more such things. Without eyes of faith, the Israelites would never have been able to understand what all these things truly meant, and so they would have derived no spiritual benefit from them at all. The mystery of God's gracious kingship would have been hidden from their eyes. But when an Israelite looked with faith at what was happening in the temple, the things he saw would reveal something of God and His glorious kingdom.

Just as the tabernacle and the items inside contained both veiled and revealed truth, so too the parables used very ordinary things to both conceal and reveal God's grace and glory. In using parables, Christ was, as it were, taking His disciples by the hand and leading them through the everyday things and situations of life into the message of the kingdom. What could seed in the earth say about the kingdom? Or a woman seeking a lost coin? An unjust steward? Virgins waiting for a wedding? In each of these cases, the ordinary first seems to veil the glorious, but then, to the humble inquirer, it also reveals it. Even Christ stoops to hide Himself in the ordinary stuff of the parables—in the sower, in the treasure in the field, in the pearl, and in the prodigal's father.

Glory Unveiled

In order to see the glory that Christ has concealed in the parables and throughout the Scriptures, we need to have our spiritual eyes opened. By the work of His Holy Spirit, the Lord needs to make us humble and teachable. We need faith to believe what we cannot understand with our fallen minds.

We need to have the darkness of our minds driven back. We need the hindrances in our hearts and lives exposed and broken down. We need to become disciples who ask the Lord to "declare unto us the parable" (Matt. 13:36).

What happens when the Lord unveils that glory? It is like what Paul pictured in 2 Corinthians 3:7–18. He refers to the time when God revealed His glory on Mount Horeb to instruct the people of Israel and to set up His kingdom among them. Many had some initial sense that something special was happening. However, they soon failed to see anything glorious about it and turned aside to wicked idolatry (Ex. 32:1). To them God's glory was concealed. But God revealed His glory to Moses, and in Moses at least, this revelation effected a change. His face shone to such an extent that he had to cover it when he returned from the mountain. When God's Word impacts us experimentally, it effects a change "from glory to glory" (2 Cor. 3:18).

How we need this glory to change us by transcribing itself upon our hearts and lives! Ultimately, this change is the work of the Holy Spirit (John 16:13–15). May He work so that when we read the parables, they indeed read and take control of us. May He search our hearts as we search the Scriptures, and thus may they have thoroughgoing effect on our heart, soul, and might (Deut. 6:5).

Questions

1. Why don't most people see the true glory of the Scriptures?

2. Read 1 Samuel 4:19–22. The wife of Phinehas understood the significance of glory and what it meant for it to be gone. What happens when churches and people treat the Bible in a way in which they don't see its glory? How does this sense of the glory of God return where it has been lost?

3. How did God veil and unveil His glory in the tabernacle? How does this compare to what He does in His Word?

4. Many people think of the parables as nice stories, illustrating lovely points of God's truth. Why is it a problem to study the parables like that?

5. Christ quoted Isaiah 6:9–10 on the great day of parables (Matt. 13:14–15). Compare what Isaiah saw in Isaiah 6 and what the people should have seen the day Christ spoke those words.

Interesting ?

6. Is it realistic to think that every time we read the Scriptures, we ought to see the glory of Christ in them?

Thumbs up

One thing to think about is that God put the parables in the Bible for a good reason,

and the reason is revealed in this book.
(or unveiled)

The King of Glory

THE MYSTERY OF THE PARABLES
(Matthew 13:10–17)

And the disciples came, and said unto him,
Why speakest thou unto them in parables? He
answered and said unto them, Because it is given
unto you to know the mysteries of the kingdom
of heaven, but to them it is not given.

—MATTHEW 13:10–11

2

Imagine this scenario that has occurred many times throughout history: A conquering king has subdued a neighboring country and banished the original king. The original king, however, sends representatives, who spread reports among his people about his plans to retake the country. Often these reports would be in code, so that if the occupying king learned about it, he would not necessarily understand all the dynamics of the plans. The message was intentionally "locked," or veiled. Nevertheless, those for whom the message was intended were able to "unlock," or unveil, the code.

Now imagine that the king himself would come, moving among his people, but hiding his identity from them, to announce the imminent return of his kingdom and how it will be accomplished. Can you imagine the momentum building and loyalties being strengthened as the disguised king himself gave firsthand reports about the coming kingdom?

This is exactly how the parables functioned in Christ's ministry. The prophets had come before, teaching the people many things about the coming king and His kingdom. But now Christ Himself was on the scene. So these familiar and appealing stories in Scripture are actually messages in code of the kingdom of heaven from the king Himself. In fact, the king Himself came veiled in flesh, announcing and explaining His one-of-a-kind kingdom.

Many did not understand what was happening. Some were repulsed by whatever they did understand about the message. Others found themselves strangely drawn to the message of these parables and to the One who was speaking them. These parables fostered a mysterious hope in them. It also exposed the emptiness of their hearts apart from this king and their rebellion, hardness, and unbelief with respect to Him. Above all, these parables drew them out of themselves and to the feet of the king, whose reign they deeply desired. Thus the parables gloriously and mysteriously were extending God's kingdom in people's hearts as they gave the message of the kingdom in code. Through them Christ was extending His kingdom and mastering many hearts.

The Scenery

We might define parables as *comparisons, with scenarios and stories drawn from everyday life in order to conceal and reveal spiritual truth relating to the kingdom of heaven.* Christ used the stuff of creation and life as it was lived every day as code for His message about the kingdom.

Think of the rich and varied scenery He used in parables. There are agricultural scenes—a sower going out to sow, or a fig tree being examined by the husbandman to see whether it is bearing fruit. There is a threshing floor. There are vines and vineyards. There is a shepherd with his sheep. There is a woman in her house. There is a wedding scene with bridesmaids waiting to attend a bride. There is a marriage banquet, where guests come dressed in wedding clothes. There is an estate on which a father lives with his two sons and hired servants. There are two men building houses in different locations—one on rock, one on the sand. There is a traveling scene where a man is attacked by robbers as he makes his way from one place to another. What common, everyday scenes! Think of Christ's use of common elements—of pearls, leaven, oil, coins, and sheep. Jesus did so much with the ordinary things of life! *– we might be able to too!*

As the Son of God, Christ had created all these things, seen and unseen. But in His human nature, He studied this glory that His own eternal hands had made. In fact, in the parables Christ harnessed the glory of His own creation and used it as the code to convey most splendidly the glory of His kingdom.

The Substance

What did Christ convey in code? The parables are not intended to teach general lessons and morals without any coherent, consistent focus. Instead, when Jesus began to teach in parables, He specifically did so in order to reveal the kingdom of God. So many of the parables begin that way. "Again, the kingdom of heaven is like…" (e.g., Matt. 13:24, 31, 33, 44, 45, 47). Moreover, when the disciples ask Christ, "Why speakest thou unto them in parables?" He answers, "Because it is given unto you to know the mysteries of the kingdom of heaven, but to them it is not given" (Matt. 13:10–11).

What is meant by "the kingdom of heaven"? This kingdom can be defined as the gracious reign of God in the hearts of His people by faith in His Son, the king of the kingdom. This kingdom is invisible to the human eye, but it operates in

Christians can see it in the lives of other Christians

hearts throughout the world and is moving to a final culmination at the second coming of Christ.

Christ did not unveil this substance all at once. When we study the parables in order, as accurately as we can reconstruct that order, we see a pattern develop. At first, Christ dealt largely with the idea of the *coming of the kingdom* in parables about such things as the sower sowing, the strong man bound, and the seed growing secretly in the earth. The gospel writer Matthew has recorded most of these parables for us. Next, Christ spoke more in depth of the *grace of the kingdom*. Think of the parables of the good Samaritan, the great supper, and the prodigal son. The gospel writer Luke has recorded most of these parables for us. Finally, as Christ approached Jerusalem, the focus of the parables shifted again—this time toward *Christ's return*, an event that would mark a radical division in the kingdom. Think of the parable of the man without the wedding garment (Matt. 22:1–14), the parable of the ten virgins (Matt. 25:1–13), and the parable of the sheep and the goats (Matt. 25:31–46).

It is also interesting to notice that the only two parables recorded in the book of John focus on Christ's revealing Himself: the parable of the sheepfold (10:1–18), and the parable of the vine and the branches (15:1–17). Certainly, all of these topics relate to the kingdom of heaven and aim to subdue our hearts and minds to its reign of grace.

The Savior

The parables are about more, however, than just the kingdom in code. Ultimately, Christ is the subject of the parables. The glory of the parables is derived from His glory as the king of the kingdom. Ultimately, He is the one who has come to sow the Word of God (Matt. 13:37). He is the one digging around the fig tree (Luke 13:8). He is the treasure in the field and the pearl of great price (Matt. 13:44, 46). He is the one who, through His messengers, is graciously inviting people to a great supper of God (Luke 14:23). He is the bridegroom, who is soon to come for His church (Matt. 25:13). He is the shepherd who goes out to find the lost sheep (Luke 15:5). Who is the father in the parable of the prodigal son, other than God through Christ looking while prodigals are still a long way off (Luke 15:20)? All the parables that speak of grace enfold Christ, at whose expense that grace will be dispensed. When by faith you look in the rearview mirror at all the parables, you realize it is the king of the kingdom whose portrait is like a watermark throughout. What rich insights there are in the parables into the person and work of the Redeemer, for those who believe!

christ *christians only*

The Searchlight

When His disciples asked Him why He taught in parables, Christ quoted Isaiah 6:9–10: "Hear ye indeed, but understand not; and see ye indeed, but perceive not. Make the heart of this people fat, and make their ears heavy, and shut their eyes; lest they see with their eyes, and hear with their ears, and understand with their heart, and convert, and be healed" (see, e.g., Matt. 13:10–17). It was when people, especially the leaders, began to reject Him and His teaching that Christ began using parables. They unveil the truth of the kingdom to believers but veil and therefore hide it from unbelievers. How do they do that?

The parables read our hearts. The glory of Christ in the parables acts like an X-ray, unmasking and exposing the evil in our hearts. When, for instance, Christ speaks in the parable of the sower of the stony ground, He is exposing the hardheartedness that is so common among hearers of the word. Think of how the parable of the rich fool exposes our greediness and selfish spirit, as we think we have our lives all in order, with many goods stored up for years. Think of how the parable of the good Samaritan indicts us for our coldness in the name of religion and our mercilessness to those in need of mercy. In these and many other instances, Christ is pointing out the need for our hearts to be changed.

The parables transcribe Christ's rule upon our hearts. Paul writes similarly in 2 Corinthians 3:3: "Ye are...written not with ink, but with the Spirit of the living God; not in tables of stone, but in fleshy tables of the heart." Often, the parables challenge us in a way that requires a response. They give directions, encouragements, or warnings. Think of the parable of the friend at midnight, which ends with these words: "Ask, and it shall be given you; seek, and ye shall find; knock, and it shall be opened unto you" (Luke 11:9). Or think of the ending to the parable of the unmerciful servant. There Christ gives us this warning: "So likewise shall my heavenly Father do also unto you, if ye from your hearts forgive not every one his brother their trespasses" (Matt. 18:35).

This is also how Christ's parables become gloriously effective in the lives of believers. Our hearts need to become places where the glory of Christ and His cross reside—like glory in earthen vessels (2 Cor. 4:7): veiled in a certain sense, and yet also reflecting the beauty and kingly glory of Christ.

Questions

1. If you had to choose a favorite parable, which would it be? Why?

2. Define the kingdom of heaven. How and why do the parables speak about the kingdom in code, or in a veiled way? Are we used to talking about the kingdom as much as Christ did?

3. Many people think of the parables almost as sermon illustrations, which simplify a spiritual point for hearers. According to Matthew 13:10–13, is this accurate?

4. A simple believer will understand a parable like an unbelieving scholar never will. Do you agree? How would that work with, for example, the parable of the two builders (Matt. 7:24–27)?

5. Nathan told David a parable in order to search his heart (2 Sam. 12:1–6). Give an example of how one of Christ's parables might function as a searchlight.

se pg 15

3ª see py. 15

The Glory of the Kingdom:
Some Parables in Matthew and Mark

The Glory of Kingdom Reception

THE PARABLE OF THE SOWER
(Mark 4:1–20)

The sower soweth the word…. And these are they which are sown on good ground; such as hear the word, and receive it, and bring forth fruit, some thirtyfold, some sixty, and some an hundred.

—MARK 4:14, 20

~ 3 ~

The gospels give the parable of the sower a prominent place in the record of Christ's ministry. Three of the gospels record it, along with the interpretation that Christ gives of it (Matt. 13:1–8; Mark 4:1–8; Luke 8:5–8). Basically, Christ uses the process of agricultural production, from sowing to harvesting, to signify the spiritual restoration that God works in grace, otherwise known as the kingdom of heaven (see Matthew 13:19, "the word of the kingdom").

Christ did not derive this agricultural theme as a symbol for the kingdom of God simply from nature. The Old Testament contains many promises of spiritual restoration, and a number of them use the imagery of seed being sown (see, e.g., Ps. 126:5–6; Jer. 31:27–28; Hos. 2:23). The prophets also used the picture of agricultural devastation to symbolize judgment (see, e.g., Isa. 34:9–15).

It is not surprising, then, that Christ uses the picture of a sower and his seed. But what is surprising is that the sower in this parable sows on four soils, with only one of them producing fruit. Christ clearly was intending to highlight the fact that the word of God does not have the same effect everywhere it is sown. Not all gospel preaching yields gospel fruit, and it is the glory of divine omniscience to uncover that.

The Scenery

The parable introduces us to a sower, seed, and various kinds of soils. It is easy to picture the scene. You don't need to be a farmer to know about the possibility that a planted seed won't sprout and the disappointment that failure would cause. There is nothing that suggests the sower of the parable is ill-equipped or unskillful at what he does. Neither is there a problem with the seed; it is not inferior or corrupt. The problem is with the various kinds of soil.

The first ground Christ portrays is the well-packed earth alongside the field, where perhaps generations of people have walked, hardening the soil until it is impervious to the seed (Mark 4:4). Christ describes hungry fowl, which devour the seed. Just a minute or two after the sower had the seed in his bag and then ran it through his hand, it disappears from the ground into the birds' beaks. The wayside is no better off, and the seed is gone forever.

Next is the stony ground (v. 5). The picture here is of a thin layer of soil under which there is dense rock. The seeds that fall here do germinate, spring up, and take root. But the roots cannot find depth of earth, and when the hot sun beats down on the little seedlings, they shrivel up and lie withered on top of the soil. This is evidence of the rocks just below the surface.

Third is the ground with thorns and thistles (v. 7). Here, the problem is that though there is soil and presumably depth, there are also thorns and thistles. Christ does not state whether these weeds are in seed form or already beginning to sprout, but eventually they choke the sprouting seed.

So Christ details a farmer's familiar nightmare. We can all imagine the farmer's pain at having expended sweat and toil, and then losing his precious seed to such unproductive ends. When we look at these three soils, we cannot help but think about how this symbolizes the misery of the fall of our first parents. There was no fruitless labor before the fall. But now, thorns, thistles, and wilted plants all attest to the fact that the heart of man itself has become an unproductive field with respect to the Lord, who is the great husbandman (literally, "farmer" [John 15:1]).

Even though the majority of the soils are ultimately unproductive, Christ finally mentions that there is also a good ground. The seed that falls into this good soil bears forth fruit to different degrees: "some thirty, and some sixty, and some an hundred" (v. 8).

The Substance

The following points are central to the message of the parable. First, Christ is showing how the restoration He brings does not have saving effect wherever it comes, yet in the end it will most certainly produce fruit. Christ's parable builds upon and fits with the prophecy in Isaiah 55:10–11: "For as the rain cometh down, and the snow from heaven, and returneth not thither, but watereth the earth, and maketh it bring forth and bud, that it may give seed to the sower, and bread to the eater: so shall my word be that goeth forth out of my mouth: it shall not return unto me void, but it shall accomplish that which I please, and it shall prosper in the thing whereto I sent it." Christ is not comparing His word to the rain, which is mentioned first in this text, but rather to the seed. Nevertheless, in both the prophecy and the parable God's word is compared to the agent effecting transformation.

Essentially, what Christ is saying is this: "As I have been preaching to you, I have been scattering the seed of the word upon the fields of Israel. Because of your sin, you became a desolate land spiritually, as your prophets abundantly made clear (Isa. 35:1). But now, in my ministry, the seed of the word is coming down on you, and this will continue in the ministry of the apostles. Even then I will be the sower from heaven through my servants and people. That is how the spiritual restoration will unfold—by the power of My word."

We can infer from Christ's teaching here that the word of God should be proclaimed far and wide, even if the seed of the word thereby falls beyond a perfectly prepared or obviously fertile ground. As the Canons of Dort put it, the word should be "declared and published to all nations, and to all persons promiscuously and without distinction" (II, 5). That is what Christ Himself did, and He commanded His apostles no differently (Matt. 28:19–20). It will often seem that much of the seed is wasted when the gospel is preached widely. Isaiah lamented, "Who hath believed our report?" (Isa. 53:1; cf. John 12:38; Rom. 10:16). But it is better for a farmer to labor, sweat, and cast the seed in places where it may not yield fruit than it is for him to assume that he knows exactly which soil is good ground (see Eccl. 11:6). So too Christ sends His word into many places and to many people where it will not ultimately yield true, saving restoration.

Second, Christ is asserting that this ministry of the word will prove which hearts are receptive to the word, and which are not. In light of the fact that Christ's parable hooks into Old Testament promises of a coming spiritual restoration, many of His hearers may have thought this parable would bring good news. If they could have written a different ending to the parable, it might have been like this: "A sower went out to sow, and everywhere he sowed, life and fruitfulness ensued, bringing prosperity and beauty and all manner of success." Many people today want to hear the same kind of news: "Christ will certainly and quickly bring good things into your life. Believe this morning, and you'll see success by evening." This parable proves differently. Only one-quarter of the ground into which the seed falls is fruitful ground. Three out of the four soils prove ultimately unreceptive to the word.

Let's trace more closely what Christ is doing by treating the different soils. As He describes the first three kinds of ground, His all-seeing eye scrutinizes more deeply into human hearts than anyone else ever could. No one knows the heart of man like He.

First, He exposes the wayside hearers. The seed stays on the surface rather than penetrating, and the devil simply takes the word away, "out of their hearts" (Luke 8:12). Can't many, if not all of us relate to this? How many times, after hearing a sermon or reading the Bible, has this happened in our hearts? The word seems to have evaporated as quickly as we heard it. Perhaps many of us will take comfort from remembering the times when the word has had some effect in our lives. Perhaps we can point out little "shoots" of new life that have sprouted up after we heard the word. But we should heed what Christ says next in this parable.

Next, Christ deals with the rocky soil. In this case, hardness of heart might not be visible on the surface, but it is only an inch or two below the surface. Although there are evidences of new life after the word is preached, Christ fast-forwards to show us how the young shoots wither under the sun of "affliction or persecution" (Mark 4:17). The cause is this: there was "no root in themselves" (Mark 4:17). Notice it is "themselves" who are to blame, for there is no root in them. Listen to how the Canons of Dort similarly incriminate some hearers of the word: "Others, though they receive it, *suffer it not* to make a lasting impression on their heart" (III–IV, 9, emphasis added). The fault clearly lies in the hearers.

Despite this second revelation from the all-seeing Savior, many professing Christians will again heave a sigh of relief, reminding themselves quickly that they have not "withered away" like others have. After all, they are still under the preaching of the gospel, and they don't consider themselves withered or rootless. So Christ's skillful eye probes deeper still as He treats the third soil.

Christ fast-forwards again and pictures the young shoots in the soil, this time surrounded by thorns and briers. These toxic plants have grown up with such a vengeance that the young plants are defenseless against them. Christ, as it were, points to the thorns and identifies them for us: "cares of this world, and the deceitfulness of riches, and the lusts of other things" (Mark 4:19). Again the Canons of Dort stress that the hearers themselves are at fault: "Others choke the seed of the word by perplexing cares, and the pleasures of this world, and produce no fruit" (III–IV, 9). No one can rest comfortably under this diagnosis. Who never feels the sting of cares, the lure of riches, and the quills of harmful desires? Who has not been guilty of choking the word by allowing other things to take priority? When you sense the truth of that, Christ's parable has had an experimental effect. You might as well ask with the disciples, "Who then can be saved?" (Mark 10:26).

Thankfully, Christ explains that there is also good ground into which the word falls. He explains what that is: "That on the good ground are they, which in an honest and good heart, having heard the word, keep it, and bring forth fruit with patience" (Luke 8:15). This is the ground on which God has so worked that there is an internal honesty, or as Psalm 51 says, "truth in the inward parts" (v. 6). There is a reception of the word to the point that, through the blessing of the Lord, it is kept, and fruit grows (Mark 4:20). Nothing like this happened in the first three kinds of soil. This is the only ground that yields a harvest. Those who have been regenerated by the Spirit of God hear the Word of God, embrace it, and bring forth fruit. It's no wonder that the Lord ended this parable with a cry: "He that hath ears to hear, let him hear" (Luke 8:8).

The Savior

As Christ speaks this parable, He reveals himself in three ways:

1. *See Him as the sovereign, or king of the kingdom of heaven, whose secrets He is revealing in parables* (Mark 4:11). As He speaks parables like this, and through the rest of His teaching as well, He is bringing in the kingdom of grace that the prophets had prophesied.

2. *See Him as the sower, who brings this restoration by His word and Spirit.* Christ loved the emblem of seed and used it frequently, not in the least because it pictured naturally what happens spiritually, namely, fruitfulness in the way of

humiliation and death. He—the sower—would ultimately become a seed, as He explains later (John 12:24). Moreover, He—the sower—would ultimately be the "good and honest" heart, as He says: "I do always those things that please him" (John 8:29). We can have a good and honest heart only because of His perfectly receptive heart to His Father. We need His payment on the cross for all our hardness of heart with respect to the Lord and His word.

3. *See Him as the omniscient surgeon, who diagnoses our spiritual heart condition through this parable and others.* Not only does He diagnose our condition, but He also addresses our hearts by His work on the cross. There He obtained the quickening Spirit whereby He renders our hearts pliable and receptive, and so effectually works upon the soil of our hearts, that we hear, receive, and bring forth fruit to His praise and glory.

The Searchlight

This parable searches our hearts regarding how we receive the word of God. Which of the soils most corresponds to our hearts? Even true believers cannot simply comfort themselves that they are "the good soil." For even after grace, believers struggle with sin and unbelief as it is pictured for us in the first three soils. The ultimate question is this: What do we do after Christ's glorious omniscience exposes our unreceptive hearts, or unreceptive tendencies in our hearts, for what they are?

The disciples here point the way. While other hearers presumably left—thereby revealing that they were not receiving the seed that Christ had just sown—the disciples went to the Lord, heeding His cry: "He that hath ears to hear, let him hear" (Luke 8:8–9). They were not offended by His words, but wanted to hear more of them.

It is important to remember, however, that Judas would have been among the disciples that day. He would prove to be a thorny-ground hearer. He allowed the powerful thorn of the deceitfulness of riches to ultimately choke the word in his life. He betrayed Christ for thirty pieces of silver. But thankfully the others, despite all the remaining sin in their lives, evidenced ultimately an "honesty before God" and received a continued work of the Sower-Savior in their hearts.

Questions

1. Christ tells us that the seed is the word (Mark 4:14). We can safely say that He is speaking of the pure, undiluted, and uncontaminated word of God. If this is true, where then are these different grounds Christ is speaking of to be found?

2. Read 2 Timothy 4:10, in which Paul makes reference to Demas. Based on what Paul writes about him, what kind of hearer was Demas, and what powerful thorn choked the word of God in his life?

3. Why didn't the sower just sow on the good ground? What can we learn from this?

4. Think about how hardships can choke the word of God. Describe how you might find that happening in your life now, or how it may have happened to you in the past.

5. Why should we not be content with a shallow Christianity? What can make the "roots" go down deep?

The Glory of Kingdom Sovereignty

THE PARABLE OF THE SEED
GROWING SECRETLY
(Mark 4:26–29)

And he said, So is the kingdom of God, as if a man should cast seed into the ground; and should sleep, and rise night and day, and the seed should spring and grow up, he knoweth not how. For the earth bringeth forth fruit of herself; first the blade, then the ear, after that the full corn in the ear. But when the fruit is brought forth, immediately he putteth in the sickle, because the harvest is come.

—MARK 4:26–29

~ 4 ~

In the spring, young children love to plant a few seeds in a cup, put the cup against a sunny window, and wait…day after day…for the thin green blades to push their way up through the soil. It is the miracle of new life, and it comes in such a mysterious way that their minds are captivated. Having to wait a week or two to see results is part of the excitement.

The lessons learned from watching and waiting as a seed germinates and a plant begins to grow are not only valuable for children. As we see in this parable, they are important lessons for all who wish to know how the kingdom of heaven takes shape.

The Scenery

Only Mark records this parable. We find it on the heels of the parable of the sower, in which Christ spoke about the preparation of the soul for the gospel message. Christ was making clear that not all hearts have been prepared to receive the gospel, so the preaching of the word does not always bear fruit.

In this parable of the growing seed, Christ is dealing with the *process* that the gospel message undergoes in the soul. The parable mentions three main stages in the process: sowing, growing, and reaping. During the sowing stage the seed was "cast," or embedded in the ground. During the second stage, the seed *grew*—first the blade; next, the ear; and then the full corn in the ear. Then, finally, there was the reaping stage, when the fruit was fully ripened.

Between casting his seed and reaping the harvest, however, the sower had no direct involvement in what was happening to the seed. It was happening secretly. The parable seems to emphasize this by saying that after casting the seed to the ground, the man in the parable slept. We read of him rising "night and day," which tells us that time was passing. The sower wasn't anxiously turning over the soil to see if he could detect any growth or pacing up and down the fields at night trying to hasten the crop's growth. On the contrary, he slept at night and rose each day to do his other tasks, simply leaving the seed to grow.

Christ draws specific attention to the fact that the farmer did not know or understand all that went into the process of the seed springing up and growing: "he knoweth not how" (v. 27). The farmer operated with an implicit confidence that there would be a harvest. He trusted that there would be a harvest even when he didn't understand all that was happening under the ground.

The Substance

The Lord had given His disciples an explicit interpretation for the parable of the sower. That probably means that the parable we are now considering may have been the first parable that these disciples—newly initiated into the mysterious world of the parables—would need to try to interpret on their own. If they listened with faith, much about the growth of the kingdom would be unveiled to them.

The basic message of this parable is found in this phrase: "for the earth bringeth forth fruit of herself" (v. 28). The Greek word translated as "of herself" is *automate*, from which the English word "automatic" comes. Christ is picking up on the fact that the growth of the plant is an automatic process, subservient to the order and laws of creation. It is the natural process of a seed, when it is cast into the earth, to bring forth a plant. This natural process is far more comprehensive than anything farmers could do by themselves; ultimately, the Creator of heaven and earth, who has designed all things and still maintains and directs them, through these means brings forth a harvest from the seed.

God's work in redemption functions similarly to His work in creation and the natural world in significant ways. As in nature, so in grace—God alone is the sovereign source of life and growth. Paul says it this way: "God…giveth the increase" (1 Cor. 3:7). Spiritual life cannot be traced out with the human hand any more than the physical growth of these corn plants was. Matthew Henry comments, "God carries on his work insensibly and without noise, but insuperably and without fail." And when God gives the increase, He does so gradually, just as we see with corn. The seed began to grow and came to fruition in steps—the blade, the ear, then the full corn in the ear. And so some in the kingdom of God are still "blades," others "ears," and still others are "full corn." A blade evidences new life, even though there is no fruit to be seen yet. Every lush corn-bearing plant was once only a sensitive blade. The ear is the next step of growth. It is the beginning of the formation of fruit, but it is not ripe and mature fruit yet.

Of course, we should not force parallelisms between natural life and spiritual life because of this parable. For example, the parable does not mean to imply that those who die quickly after conversion, in the "blade" or "ear" stage of spiritual life, would fail to bring forth a full measure of fruit to the glory of God. God measures and gauges fruit according to His standard, and we cannot understand that standard with our human minds. God's harvest of each plant is perfectly and divinely timed—and never comes a moment too early or too late.

The Savior

Many interpreters have unintentionally confirmed that Christ here has veiled His glory, since they have difficulty seeing the sower of this parable as Christ. They cite the apparent discrepancy that the sower did not know how the seed sprang up and grew (v. 27). Yet if Christ were not the sower, neither would He be the reaper, for verse 29 says, "Immediately he [that is, the sower] putteth in the sickle, because the harvest is come." We know that Christ is ultimately both the sower and the reaper. And so we regard this farmer's "not knowing how" his seed was growing as being an earthly element of the story.

In the end, the point is precisely that Christ is much more than just the sower. In His incarnation, He took on a true human nature in order that He could come to this world and personally sow the message of the kingdom. As the second person of the divine Trinity, He also has all the power necessary to make the seed He sows grow. Through His life, death, and resurrection, He exerts a power equivalent to that of creating the universe as He regenerates people. Through the power of His Spirit, He makes them grow up in Him. Paul says it this way: "If we have been planted together in the likeness of his death, we shall be also in the likeness of his resurrection" (Rom. 6:5). In the covenant of redemption, He has been given people to sow, grow, and reap—all to the glory of God.

Later on the same day that Christ told this parable, an event transpired that confirms this point. We read about the great miracle of Christ in calming a terrible storm, in which it seems like all of nature's power is in force against the disciples (Mark 4:35–51). But if the disciples had had Christ's parable fresh on their minds, they would perhaps not have been surprised to find Christ sleeping on the ship. After all, like the sower of the parable, He had completed His day of sowing, and now He could sleep, confident that His word would not return void, but accomplish what He purposed (Isa. 55:10).

So then Christ, the sower who can sleep confidently, explains the next moment why He can sleep. He proves that even earth's fiercest powers are under His control. In other words, "the earth" in which the seed grows is under the control of this human and divine sower. The growth of the kingdom is not left simply to natural laws; the Lord Jesus divinely directs nature. This is the glory Christ unveils to the eyes of faith. Though hidden in the ground, unseen by human eyes, the seed is still taken care of, cultivated, and nourished by Him who sits enthroned over all creation. Precisely through these storms, He is growing the seed of faith in His people's lives, until the growth reaches the stage He desires for it (see Eph. 4:14–15).

The Searchlight

This parable is useful in examining ourselves on at least three points:

1. *Self-reliance.* Often we get bogged down with the latest trends, methods, and strategies, thinking they will produce spiritual growth in ourselves or others. We may try to grow the seed in our children or friends or neighborhoods, even working tirelessly as we do so. We may be trying to work up some growth in our lives through self-improvement or self-discipline. The confident sleep of the farmer in the parable proves how vain our self-reliance can be.

2. *Faith.* Instead of relying on ourselves, do we rest in the gracious providence and covenant of God? Indeed, we are called upon to sow the seed of God's Word in the lives of our children, friends, and neighbors. However, do we carry on with our day-to-day business as we do so, confident that the mighty work of regeneration is God's work, and what He begins, He will finish? The life of faith is a life lived trusting in Jesus Christ. It is by faith that we must continue, even in the times that seem spiritually to be the driest and most uneventful.

3. *Growth.* We can't read this parable without asking these questions: Which stage am I in? Has fruit started to show itself in my life? Or is it perhaps true that my life does not so much as show a blade of new life?

As the searchlight of this parable reads us, we need Christ from heaven to decrease our self-reliance and increase our faith. We are not the shapers of our own destiny. Instead, we need to learn to be content to be seed on His earth, which, from heaven, He is growing through His almighty grace.

Questions

1. So often when the Bible tells us to *believe*, we want to *behold*. Discuss how the parable should convict us on this point.

2. The Bible speaks elsewhere about various levels of faith (weak faith, strong faith, great faith, etc.). Trace how the disciples' faith might have developed throughout their lives along the three stages (blade, ear, mature corn in the ear).

3. After telling this parable, Christ takes the disciples onto the Sea of Galilee (Mark 4:35–41). There Christ sleeps while the disciples fret. How does this parable of the seed growing shed light on growth in the life of the disciples?

4. Small beginnings often discourage us. How does this parable remind us that they should not? Why do you think God often chooses to work in the way of small beginnings?

The Glory of Kingdom Patience

THE PARABLE OF THE TARES
(Matthew 13:24–30, 36–43)

The servants said unto him, Wilt thou then that we go and gather them up? But he said, Nay; lest while ye gather up the tares, ye root up also the wheat with them. Let both grow together until the harvest: and in the time of harvest I will say to the reapers, Gather ye together first the tares, and bind them in bundles to burn them: but gather the wheat into my barn.

—MATTHEW 13:28–30

Most of us know how frustrating it is to deal with weeds. Perhaps you've planted a vegetable or flower garden, only to find rather quickly that the weeds were more numerous than the plants you were expecting to see sprout from the ground. Perhaps you looked out over the weeds and wondered whether the painstaking and backbreaking labor of trying to pick them out would be worth it. But the problem that presents itself in this story, the parable of the tares, is more serious yet. As the tares sprouted and grew, they looked practically identical to the wheat alongside them. It was nearly impossible to identify them correctly. Only at harvest time would the differences between the wheat and the tares become obvious.

The Scenery

Matthew is the only gospel writer who includes the parable of the tares. It is the second in a series of seven parables that deal with the mystery of the kingdom of heaven (Matt. 13:11). This parable and the parable of the sower are the only ones among all the parables for which Christ gives an explicit explanation (vv. 36–43).

Like the parable of the sower, this parable begins by introducing us to a sower and his seed. But Christ speaks now of good *seed*, as opposed to a good *soil* (Matt. 13:24; see Matt. 13:8). The farmer sowed good wheat seed on his field, but then, at night, his enemy came and over-sowed the wheat with bad seed. *Competitors in ancient times would do this.*

Christ uses the word "tares" to describe this bad seed. As an expert in botany has explained, the tare is not a weed, but rather a far inferior and unusable member of the same family of grasses that includes wheat. As it grows, it is virtually indistinguishable from wheat. Only its leaf size is different by a few millimeters. You can clearly tell the difference only near the time of the harvest, and the useless (some say even poisonous) kernel appears.

According to the parable, there is a point when the servants of the master did recognize what the enemy had done (v. 27). They suggested to their master that they try to separate out the wheat from the tares. He responded, "Nay; lest while ye gather up the tares, ye root up also the wheat with them. Let both grow together until the harvest" (vv. 29–30). It's clear from the householder's answer that only in the final stages of growth would there be enough difference between the wheat and the tares that the reapers could separate the two accurately and effectively. Until then, the two had to grow up together.

The Substance

It is important to notice how the parable opens: "The kingdom of heaven is likened…" (Matt. 13:24). Some people have been confused by Christ's explanation later that the field is the world, and assume that this parable therefore teaches that there are both good and bad people in the world at large.

Though that is true, Christ is here focused on the kingdom in the world, in other words, on the visible church. The way in which God through Christ brings His reign of grace into this world (the field) could be compared to sowing.

Notice that in this parable the seed is not the word of God (as it was in the parable of the sower), but the people whom God has regenerated through His Spirit by means of His word (1 Peter 1:23; James 1:18). Christ tells us that the "good seed are the children of the kingdom" (v. 38). They have the good heart (Luke 8:15), which God alone can give through the miracle of the rebirth. This comparison was also used in Hosea, where God speaks of His people and says, "I will sow her unto me in the earth" (Hos. 2:23). This is the first aspect of the kingdom in the world, namely, the true children of the kingdom.

But there is also bad seed, which grows up as tares. Christ explains that these tares are "the children of the wicked one" (v. 38). Christ is speaking about more than just the mystery of the kingdom. He is explaining what Scripture elsewhere calls "the mystery of iniquity" (2 Thess. 2:7). Contrary to what many imagine, the kingdom of God does not come in one sweeping development. Instead, there is "an enemy" (v. 28) who interferes with the growth of the wheat. Satan is the wicked imitator of the Lord. He tries to parallel what the Lord does, but does so through evil means and to evil ends. He comes under the cover of night. That means it's impossible to know and see exactly what he has done. Often the results of his work can be seen only after much time has passed.

Christ's parable, then, is taking the entire history of the world and compressing it into one agricultural cycle of sowing and reaping. All those in the visible church from all times and places are in this field. There are tares as well as wheat, unregenerate as well as regenerate, Esaus as well as Jacobs, the reprobate as well as the elect, hypocrites as well as true believers.

At first, it may be that there is no apparent difference between all these plants on the field of the visible church. The good and bad seed grow up together. People come into your church, and everything seems well. But perhaps the devil has brought them in under the cover of night. Others grow up in the church, and everything seems to be going well with them. But again, perhaps the devil has brought them in under the cover of night. In the end they will be reckoned only as tares. The point is this: within the visible church this mixture will always exist, and it is humanly impossible to accurately sort the two groups out from each other.

Throughout the history of the kingdom, there has always been the tendency to want to put in the sickle of judgment before the allotted time. How often have church leaders or other Christians, like the servants in the parable, not been too hasty in judgment and in their desire to purge the church? So often we want to rid ourselves of those whom we consider a blight on the kingdom of God. Two of Christ's own disciples, James and John, once asked Christ, "Wilt thou that we command fire to come down from heaven, and consume them, even as Elias did?" (Luke 9:54). If the householder of the parable had let his servants do what they wanted, they might indeed have gotten rid of some of the tares. But likely they would have missed plenty as well. More importantly, they would have pulled up some of the wheat with the tares.

The householder's primary concern here is that none of the wheat be lost. After all, the tares do not *hurt* the wheat; they *obscure* it—and only for a time. God will ensure that not a single stalk of wheat will be mistaken as a tare in the end, no matter how mixed up the two are in the field.

The Savior

Christ unveils His glory in the parable in several ways. See Him as the source of His people. He sows His people in the field of this world that they might live forever to the glory and praise of God. Nothing of His work will be lost, for in the end the righteous shall "shine forth as the sun in the kingdom of their Father" (v. 43). It's important to notice how this parable puts the work of Christ first. Before the enemy can do anything, Christ sows His people. And Satan cannot undo what Christ has done. He cannot *consume* the seed of Christ. He only can *confuse* the people of God (for a time) by trying to copy what the Lord does and working deceit.

See Him as the one who exposes Satan's devices. It is He who helps His people understand "the mystery of iniquity." Notice that in the parable the servants do not know where the tares could have come from. The householder needs to explain that the enemy has sown them (v. 28). Sometimes we wonder why so many bad things happen in the church: corruption, abuse, strife, dissension, and so on. As a result we can sometimes even wonder whether the visible church is indeed God's work. Shouldn't we expect the church to be all neat and tidy if it is truly the Lord's work? Instead, Christ here reveals that it's precisely *because* the church is God's work that the devil comes alongside and sows his evil seed as well.

See Him as the patient protector of His people. The comfort of the parable is that Christ does not need to depend on His servants to root out the problem of the tares. Instead, He has come to destroy the works of the devil (1 John 3:8). He did so principally on the cross, and He will do so in a final way at the end of time. He will do it at a time and in a way in which none of His own work will be ruined.

What glory is there in the divine patience! He allows the wicked and the righteous to coexist until the full harvest is ready. He so loves His own work that He endures the work of Satan up to a point that will most magnificently display His own glory. Paul describes the Lord's patience this way: "What if God, willing to shew his wrath, and to make his power known, endured with much longsuffering the vessels of wrath fitted to destruction?" (Rom. 9:22). What patience and care on the part of the Savior!

The Searchlight

The parable searches us on at least three specific points:

1. *Do we have and use the heavenly insight God gives in His Word on our problems?* The appearance of the tares was a riddle to the master's servants. Their master explained to them where those tares had come from and what should be done with them. Just as the servants needed their master's perspective on what was happening in the field, so we need the Lord's perspective. We need insight from Him about the perplexing problems and riddles in our lives. We need to listen to what He has said about the presence of evil in our lives, in the church, and in the world. We need His perspec-

tive on His purposes. Are we praying for wisdom from God to know and understand what is going on around us?

2. *Do we exercise a heavenly patience with respect to evil around us?* The servants in this parable needed the same patience as their master. Just because there is wickedness on every side and things seem to be getting worse rather than better doesn't mean that God's purposes will fail. We need patience in order to do what God commands and wait to inherit the full promise when He wants us to have it (see Heb. 10:36). Christians are people whose hearts are directed to patiently wait for the full fulfillment of God's purposes (see 2 Thess. 3:5).

3. *Do we nurture a heavenly hope that one day all will be set right?* This is the flipside of the coin of our need for patience. Believers can take encouragement from the vast difference between the final destination of the wheat and the final destination of the tares. For many weeks, the tares grew in harmony with the wheat, with perhaps even their roots intertwined. But the day came when they were perfectly separated, and every stalk of good wheat ended up safely in the master's barn. May we long for the day when the mixture of tares and wheat will be over and when the righteous will shine brightly in the kingdom of God (v. 43).

Questions

1. There are similarities as well as differences between this parable and the parable of the sower (Matt. 13:1–8). When you read the parable of the tares, if you are afraid you do not belong to God's people, how might the parable of the sower help you?

2. "Let both grow together" (v. 30). Could this be contradictory to what Christ teaches elsewhere in Matthew about church discipline (Matt. 18:18–19)? How then can we properly apply verse 30 of this parable to the church?

3. Find other passages that also show how patiently Christ endures the mixture of "wheat and tares" in His church. What do these passages teach us about having more patience with the imperfections and inadequacies that we see in the church around us?

4. What practical lessons can we learn from this parable about how Satan works? What other things does Scripture tell us about Satan's schemes or devices?

The Glory of Kingdom Power

THE PARABLES OF THE
MUSTARD SEED AND THE LEAVEN
(Matthew 13:31–33)

Another parable put he forth unto them, saying, The kingdom of heaven is like to a grain of
mustard seed.... Another parable spake he unto
them; the kingdom of heaven is like unto leaven.
—MATTHEW 13:31, 33

These two parables are part of an entire chapter of parables. So far in Matthew 13, each parable has taught something about the kingdom of heaven. First there was the famous parable of the sower. There Christ declares that the kingdom comes by the word of God taking root in believers' hearts, growing, and bearing fruit. In many other people, the word of God does not bring forth fruit (vv. 1–9). Next comes the parable of the tares, in which Christ makes clear that the visible kingdom will remain a mixture of good and bad until His return on the clouds and the final separation of the righteous and the wicked (vv. 24–30). There was more for His followers to learn about the kingdom, however, and so Christ continues His teaching in the parables of the mustard seed and the leaven. Through these two parables, Christ shows His disciples the remarkable, invisible power revealed in the growth of the kingdom through the gospel. He compares this power to two very familiar things—mustard seed and leaven.

The Scenery

The mustard seed is miniscule, about the size of the tip of a pencil lead. Your eye would scarcely notice it. Were a mustard seed to fall on you, you might not even take the effort to brush it off—it's that small. A bird looking for seeds to eat might miss this tiny seed and move on to something larger, such as a sunflower seed. But if this mustard seed falls into the soil and if rain and sun nurture it, a month or two later you might see a remarkable bush that has grown from that very small seed. How is that possible? When it was a seed, it looked like nothing. It seemed worthless and lifeless. But after it has nestled in the soil and received sun and water, there has been remarkable growth. The bird that didn't notice the seed before might soon find this bush a good place to build its nest.

The leaven of Bible times was not the same as the yeast we use in baking today. What Christ refers to would have been a piece of fermented dough from a previous baking, which a woman would knead into a new batch of dough. Imperceptibly, the leaven would move throughout the whole dough, powerfully impacting all of it and making it rise.

Sometimes the Bible uses the picture of leaven for something evil, such as "the leaven of the Pharisees" (Luke 12:1) or "the leaven of malice and wickedness" (1 Cor. 5:8). Evil can indeed move imperceptibly and powerfully. However, in this passage, Christ is not referring to something evil; He is again referring to the kingdom of heaven and its growth within individuals throughout the world.

The Substance

The kingdom of God may look as insignificant, worthless, and lifeless to the casual observer as the mustard seed does. We might be tempted to pass over it in our thinking and instead dwell on things more substantial and eye-catching—things like earthly governments, the media, popular trends, political figures, and human institutions.

The same would have been true of the kingdom of God in Christ's time. If you had lived then, perhaps your attention would have been focused on the Roman government as it controlled the then-known world. Uprisings, taxes, political intrigue—many such things would have seemed a lot more significant than a wandering rabbi from the back country of Galilee with a band of twelve followers. Yet, in the book of Acts, we see that kingdom growing fast and furiously in a way that matches the growth of the bush that comes from a mustard seed.

Christ wants to teach another aspect of the kingdom of God and its growth. So how does the kingdom of heaven work like leaven? We can see several similarities.

First, its work is hidden from view. The process of leavening cannot be seen with the human eye. Neither can the growth of the kingdom of God in a person's heart. The Spirit changes a heart of stone into a heart of flesh, making it soft and pliable. Although the effects of His work will indeed become visible, this radical transformation is in itself mysterious and invisible.

Another way the kingdom of heaven is like leaven is it changes from the inside out. Christ accused the Pharisees (Luke 11:39) of cleaning only the outside of their "cup," while the inside remained dirty. Their lives might have seemed righteous on the outside, but their hearts remained unclean and evil. This is not how the kingdom of God works in the heart. Like leaven working from the inside out, the changed heart brings forth a changed life (Prov. 4:23).

Finally, it works a comprehensive change in the end. Leaven makes the whole loaf rise. It makes it light and airy and tasty throughout; not one bit of loaf is left unaffected. Likewise, someone whose heart has been affected by the gospel will ultimately show in his whole life that a change has taken place. It's true that, on this side of eternity, the believer will still continue to be plagued by sin, since there are still two principles at work in his life. Yet the growth of the kingdom within him will affect all of him: his thoughts, his habits, his actions, his words, his pursuits, his priorities—in short, his life as a whole will be dramatically changed.

The Savior

Christ unveils His glory in these parables as it pertains especially to His power. Just as the mustard seed and leaven are seemingly insignificant, Christ came into this world in a way that was seemingly insignificant. Like Nathanael, many would have said, "Can there come any good thing out of Nazareth?" (John 1:46). Moreover, how many throughout the Roman Empire noticed what happened one Passover outside of Jerusalem, when Christ was crucified between two thieves, with all His followers scattered and offended? Don't you think what happened there seemed like a little, dark mustard seed compared to things that must have appeared more important? What significant change could be expected to come out of a tomb in a garden just outside Jerusalem? What lasting good could come out of Galilean fishermen spreading the news about things they saw and heard?

Yet when we survey the growth of God's kingdom since Christ's death, what a gigantic "bush" has grown up! By faith, believers can see the glory of divine power unveiled in these parables. Because of Christ, the kingdom continues to spread, over lands and nations, across oceans and deserts.

People from every corner of the earth have seen this "bush" branch out in front of them, and, like birds, many have found a place to hide and shelter among its branches—all from a single, miniscule "mustard seed" planted in the soil outside of Jerusalem long ago.

Moreover, Christ works in hearts and lives from the inside out. By His powerful Holy Spirit, He effects a comprehensive change in the lives of His people and throughout this world. No other king or kingdom can match what this glorious Son of God can do.

The Searchlight

Both these parables search our hearts to see whether we have experienced this remarkable kingdom principle operating in our lives. They also demand that we adjust and align our expectations of the kingdom of God in two ways that fit what Christ is teaching through these pictures of the mustard seed and leaven:

1. *They urge us not to despise the day of small things.* The kingdom of Christ will have its course. It doesn't come with an outward show, but with an inward power. We would do well to remember this principle as we long to see fruits of the Spirit's work in our children or in those around us with whom we have been sharing the gospel. Just because we don't see anything happening on the surface doesn't necessarily mean that nothing is going on below the surface. Let's continue to pray earnestly that the Spirit of God would do His mysterious, invisible work. If He will, then fruits of that work will become visible in time.

2. *They urge us to adore the secret work of God.* The Spirit's work in each heart is mysterious and powerful; it reaches where nothing else can reach. In the secret depths of sinful hearts, God implants a new principle that radically changes people in every possible way. The growth of God's kingdom in people's hearts affects all sorts of backgrounds and situations. Even the most hardened sinners, like the unconverted Saul of Tarsus, cannot resist this powerful, secret work of God. Has this change been worked deep in the recesses of our hearts? Do our lives pass on the leaven of the gospel in our families and communities?

Questions

1. Review what the kingdom of heaven is. Is it the same as the church? Why is Christ teaching about the kingdom in parables?

2. Give an example from church history or even your own personal life of how a small or insignificant event grew to be something spiritually significant in the kingdom of heaven.

3. What lessons do these two parables give us regarding the importance of faith, as well as the power of unbelief?

4. Matthew 17:20 refers to faith the size of a mustard seed. Describe this faith. What similarities are there to the seed in this chapter?

5. Leaven works by mixture. Apply this principle to the means of grace for ourselves, as well as evangelism to others. How does this relate to being in the world, and yet not of it?

6. I read this somewhere: "Don't judge your day from how much harvest you reap, but how many seeds you sow." How can you apply these parables practically to your family or calling in life?

The Glory of Kingdom Excellence

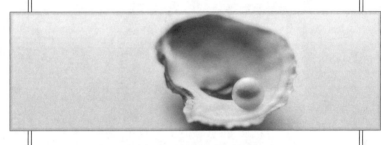

THE PARABLES OF THE TREASURE AND THE PEARL
(Matthew 13:44–46)

Again, the kingdom of heaven is like unto treasure hid in a field; the which when a man hath found, he hideth, and for joy thereof goeth and selleth all that he hath, and buyeth that field.

Again, the kingdom of heaven is like unto a merchant man, seeking goodly pearls: who, when he had found one pearl of great price, went and sold all that he had, and bought it.

—MATTHEW 13:44–46

~ 7 ~

Each of the parables in Matthew 13 deals with an aspect of the kingdom of heaven. Remember, this kingdom can be described as *the gracious reign of God in the hearts of His people by faith in His Son, the king of the kingdom.* The parables of the mustard seed and the leaven, which we already looked at, demonstrated the glory of divine power (Matt. 13:32–33). Now, the parables of the treasure in the field and the pearl of great price hone in on the preciousness, or superb excellence, of the kingdom and the king Himself.

It's noteworthy that Christ told these two parables to His disciples after He sent the multitudes away, which shows that He meant these parables to be especially for them. He desired to open up the preciousness of the kingdom particularly to His closest followers.

The Scenery
These two parables are alike in certain ways and different in others. Both deal with a treasure of surpassing excellence. Both picture someone who has an all-consuming love for the treasure and is willing to sell everything to have it. The treasure's value is beyond compare.

In the first parable, however, the man *stumbled upon* the treasure. In the second, the merchant man *sought diligently for* pearls, though in the end he found something even better than what he was expecting to find. He was looking for "goodly" (or valuable) pearls and found one of "great price," one that was extremely valuable.

We are not told much about the man who found the treasure in the field. Some think that Christ may have meant a farmer plowing a field or a traveler who stumbles on the treasure as he walks through the field. In those days, when banks weren't available, those who had reason to hide their riches would do so in an earthen vessel, placed in a location known only to them. If they died unexpectedly, their treasure would remain hidden, only to be perhaps discovered sometime in the future, usually by accident. This man sold all he had in order to buy this field and thus come to own the treasure as well.

Christ is a bit more specific about the pearl merchant. He pictures a man who possessed expert knowledge of pearls and traveled widely to the large markets in the cities of his day. Pearls were considered to be the stuff of royalty, so this merchant would have moved in elite circles. During Christ's time on earth, pearl harvesting was very difficult and dangerous. Apparently, this merchant was skilled in detecting the best pearls, those that were free from any defects or imperfections. Christ does not tell us where and how this merchant found the "pearl of great price." However, we do know that the pearl overwhelmed him with its unsurpassed beauty. The sheer eminence of the pearl made the man sell everything he had to buy it instead.

The Substance
These two parables were directed at the disciples to teach them that the value of the kingdom of heaven far exceeds the

value of anything we might own in this world. Those who part with everything they previously considered valuable in exchange for the kingdom are truly wise. After all, the worth of the kingdom transcends any and every cost. When we break this down we see three things:

1. *Many are ignorant of the excellence of the kingdom.* The kingdom of God is not something that everyone possesses. It is like treasure hidden in the field or a pearl found one day at a market. We are not born with the treasure of God in our hands. In fact, we acquire many substitute treasures, and, unless God shows us that they are substitute treasures, we are happy with them. We live out our days with far less than we could have, but are ignorant of what we are missing.

2. *When God brings us to discover the kingdom, we discern its excellence rightly.* Something can have value, but we need to understand its value and rightly estimate that value in relationship to other things. The most beautiful diamond could pass under my eye, and I might not value it any more than I would a cup of coffee. This doesn't mean that the diamond is not valuable. It only means that I don't understand how to accurately assess the value of diamonds.

Spiritually speaking, we are born with a wrong value system. We are not able to accurately assess the value of things. We prize the things of the world above the things of God. But the illuminating work of the Holy Spirit in our hearts causes us to see value where we never saw it before; what we formerly valued is soon seen to be useless, or at least far inferior to the kingdom of God. For example, the Holy Spirit brought Paul to the point where his genealogy and law-keeping became as worthless as "dung" and where he saw that the thing he had tried to destroy was actually the most valuable thing in all the world (Phil. 3:1–8).

3. *When we know the true excellence of the kingdom, everything else loses value.* Both these parables help us to understand that the intrinsic worth of the kingdom makes its cost more than worth it. Of course, we cannot purchase grace; it is without money and without price (Isa. 55:1–2). Yet it costs us everything. We cannot hold on to the substitute treasures as well as the true treasure. Just as the pearl in the parable is explicitly identified as "one" (Matt. 13:46), so we cannot serve God and mammon. We cannot have both the kingdom of heaven and the kingdom of this world.

For the believer, the "costliness" of the kingdom of God brings only blessing, for all substitutes are exposed as only substitutes, and all false allegiances are exchanged for the only allegiance that matters. The exceeding great value of the treasure made everything the man in the field owned pale in comparison. The unsurpassed value of the pearl made every other pearl dispensable in the merchant's eyes, for the sake of attaining this pearl. Like Moses, the believer comes to esteem "the reproach of Christ greater riches than the treasures in Egypt" (Heb. 11:26).

By contrast, the rich young ruler went away sorrowfully when he was told to relinquish his tight hold on his riches in exchange for the life of following Christ (Luke 18:23). This only showed that he had not truly discerned the value of the kingdom. He could not endure its cost.

The Savior

Not only does Christ *reveal* the value of the kingdom; He *represents* and *enfolds* that value in Himself. It is right that interpreters throughout the ages have understood the treasure in the field and the pearl of great price as essentially the Lord Jesus Christ. In Him are "hid all the treasures of wisdom and knowledge" (Col. 2:3). It is because of Him and in Him that the kingdom of God is a kingdom of grace. No price tag can be put on the redemption by His blood, which is more than gold and silver that perishes (1 Peter 1:18–19). To believers, Christ is precious above all (1 Peter 2:7). It's only a testimony to the blindness of fallen man that he does not see any beauty in the Savior (Isa. 53:2).

It's astounding to think that Christ left all the treasures He had in the glories of heaven in order to buy back His fallen and wretched people. He became so poor that He was content to be buried in a field in Joseph of Arimathea's tomb, in order that all who believe in Him through His poverty might be made exceedingly rich (2 Cor. 8:9).

By His Spirit, He opens our eyes to see the attractiveness of His person and work. It overpowers and overwhelms us to the point that we are willing to sacrifice all the things we previously held dear in order to apprehend that for which we have been apprehended (Phil. 3:12). Ultimately, the unsurpassed beauty of Christ is what weans us away from the substitute treasures and pearls and makes us willing to lose all, even our lives, in order to possess—rather, *be possessed by*—this treasure, Christ Jesus.

The Searchlight

These parables search our aims, actions, and affections. Have we been mesmerized by the glory and beauty of Christ to the point that we are willing to lose all we hold dear, if only we may possess Christ for time and eternity? Sadly, even many professing Christians have a lot of "selling" to do. We need to lose our sins as well as our self-righteousness. We need to be done with our love for this world and all that it holds before us. We need to put our substitutes on a heap and sign away our title to these things through and for the sake of the blood of Christ. Too often, we are too enamored by our versions of Christianity rather than with the treasure that Christ Himself is.

Questions

1. Why do you think Christ told two very similar parables? Is there any significance in the fact that the one man *stumbled* upon treasure, while the other was *seeking* it? Do these represent two different kinds of conversion?

2. Do Christians literally need to sell everything they have? Discuss what some substitutes for true treasure our hearts often pursue.

3. Notice how the rich young ruler (Matt. 19:16–22) and Paul (Phil. 3:1–11) differ in their response to the demands of Christ. Relate their responses to these parables.

4. Using what you know about pearls, discuss how Christ can be compared to the "pearl of great price."

The Glory of Kingdom Judgment

THE PARABLE OF THE NET
(Matthew 13:47–52)

Again, the kingdom of heaven is like unto a net, that was cast into the sea, and gathered of every kind: which, when it was full, they drew to shore, and sat down, and gathered the good into vessels, but cast the bad away. So shall it be at the end of the world.

—MATTHEW 13:47–49a

~ 8 ~

The parable of the net is the seventh parable in Matthew 13. How appropriate that this parable deals with the final judgment. The previous parables have all dealt with something of the mysterious beginning and growth of the kingdom. A final day is coming, however, in which everything in that kingdom will be tested, and the good separated from the bad. That is what this parable proclaims.

The Scenery

The parable paints a picture of a dragnet that caught all kinds of fish. The net was then unloaded on the shore, and the fish were sorted. The good fish were stored in vessels, while the bad were thrown away.

As is the case today, fishing in Bible times could be done in different ways. When Christ instructed Peter to catch a fish and look in its mouth for a coin, He referred to the kind of fishing that would be done with a line and a hook (Matt. 17:27). A second method was the use of a casting net—a circular net with a cord that would close the opening and trap the fish. This was the method Peter and Andrew were using when Christ called them to follow Him (Matt. 4:18). A third way of fishing is referred to in this parable. The dragnet referred to in the text is known today as a trawl net. In

Christ's time, the spread of these long and wide nets could reach up to half a mile. They would be attached behind one or more boats. The top of the net would have floats attached to it, while the bottom would have weights. As the boats moved through the water, the dragnet would catch everything in its way. Silently, almost imperceptibly, the net passed through the water and gathered fish. Most of the time, these nets would be in a certain spot only momentarily. They moved at the determination of the vessel's captain. It might be "here today, gone tomorrow." Such a net could bring in a huge variety of fish—big or small, living or dead, clean or unclean.

Next, Christ depicts the net coming to shore and the fishermen sorting the good fish into containers. The bad fish were simply discarded. This scene would have been very familiar to those listening to these parables. Even children probably regularly watched fishermen of their village sit down next to their catch and sort it in this way.

The Substance

What is the main message that Christ wants to teach us by way of this parable? Its opening sentence makes clear that Christ is giving us a picture of one aspect of the "kingdom of heaven" (v. 47). Remember that we could define this kingdom as *the gracious reign of God in the hearts of His people by faith in His Son, the king of the kingdom.* One thing to keep in mind, however, is that as God's kingdom is extended on earth, not all people visibly being gathered into it are truly part of it. People may claim to belong to the kingdom and not be real subjects of its king, the Lord Jesus. Just as the first parable in this chapter shows that only one of the four soils produced good fruit, so this parable shows that there are "good fish" and "bad fish" in the visible manifestation of the kingdom.

At the Lord's behest, the gospel moves through the world by the preaching of the word and other means of grace. It is sometimes as quiet and imperceptible as a net moving through water. It causes an initial separation, as souls are gathered into the visible church like fish into the net. Those gathered in include not only true subjects of the kingdom, but also others like Judas, Ananias and Sapphira, and Demas. These hypocrites may appear to be in the kingdom, but the kingdom is not in them.

There are essentially two separations in this parable: the first was made in the water by the net, and the second happened on the shore. Christ explains clearly what the separation on the shore refers to. "So shall it be at the end of the world: the angels shall come forth, and sever the wicked from among the just" (v. 49). This separation will take place at the end of time. Notice that He speaks of the good and bad fish as "the just" and "the wicked," respectively. This is not simply a division between people who are inherently good and inherently bad. Since "all have sinned" (Rom. 3:23), there would be only one good—Jesus Christ Himself, the only sinless one—and everyone else would be cast away. On the basis of the rest of Scripture, we can say that "the just" are those who have been declared righteous by God, by a true and living faith (see Rom. 5:9). These just were as wicked as the rest of humanity by nature. But they have been acquitted before the court of God on the basis of Christ's sacrifice on the cross, offered on their behalf. They are redeemed from the curse of the law, and this will become apparent on the day of judgment.

Christ specifically mentions the angels in the parable. One of the tasks assigned to them is the dividing between believers and unbelievers at the judgment (see Matt. 13:41; 25:31–32). As faithful, holy, and spiritual beings, they will discharge their duty swiftly and exactly. They will separate according to God's standard. What a perfect separation that will be! Not one wicked person will make it into heaven; not one of God's saved people will accidentally be lost in hell. No person will be allowed to contradict this separation and to plead his own case. All that matters is what orders the Lord has given to the angels. This is the substance of what Christ was teaching in this parable.

The Savior

Christ is unveiling Himself in this parable in terms of the glory of the divine judgment. See Him here as the one who understands the seriousness of the judgment and the final separation. He relays it to us here in order that we would know that it is not enough simply to hear His parables. It is not enough to profess to belong to a community that is set apart by the words of Christ. We need to flee for mercy to the one telling this parable. The "just" will avoid hell because of the perfect righteousness of Christ, who has endured hell for them. What glory there is in this king of the kingdom who is speaking here!

Many think the doctrine of hell goes against the idea of the love of God and the compassion of the Savior. However, the Lord Jesus spoke more about hell than anyone else in the

Bible. He addressed it in the day of grace, urging us to flee to Him while there is yet time to do so. What parent would never warn his children of fire—how hot it is and how fatal it can be? Christ warns us as the one who would suffer hell for each one of His people.

Some people think that we should not seek the Lord only because we are afraid of hell. But if the Lord sanctifies the doctrine of hell to us so that we flee from the wrath to come, let it be the first step away from the precipice of hell and into the arms of the glorious Savior, who gives His people an eternal future in heaven with Him.

The Searchlight

There are a number of ways in which this parable searches our hearts. It puts to us the following three questions:

1. *Are we content merely to be among the professing people of God?* There are untold numbers of people who are content to be in the net. They look at those outside the professing church and pride themselves that they are comfortably heading into the future. They think all is well simply because they are among other professing Christians and believe that they are all heading to heaven together. But Paul warned the Corinthians, "Examine yourselves, whether ye be in the faith; prove your own selves. Know ye not…that Jesus Christ is in you, except ye be reprobates?" (2 Cor. 13:5). This is what Christ is warning us of in this parable.

2. *Do we see ourselves as God sees us?* The great dividing line between the two groups of fish was good and bad (literally, clean and unclean). God is not concerned about what we are concerned about—things like outward appearance. His

eye sees the slightest trace of inner defilement. By nature, we are spiritually dead, and God looks at us as we would look at dead and rotting fish, and even worse. While still in this life, we need to begin to see ourselves as God sees us, and we need to value what He values. The Bible makes clear that without holiness, no man shall see the Lord (Heb. 12:14). When God works in our lives by His Spirit, He shows us something of the fountain of uncleanness within our hearts; when we see this, we turn away in horror. We begin to question: "Is that how I truly am?" But then He shows us His dear Son, who was "holy, harmless, undefiled" (Heb. 7:26), and we begin to understand what God's standard is. He then also begins to show us that, through faith in His well-beloved Son, we can receive all we need in order to be justified and sanctified. He does something that never happens in the world of fish: an unclean, defiled, dead sinner is renewed and remade after the image of Jesus Christ. Jesus Christ went through death and the judgment of God in order to forever remove wrath and judgment from His people. Do we value God's Son? Do we value His righteousness and holiness?

3. *Do we reckon with the truth of hell?* Hell is a doctrine that many have tried to eliminate from the Bible. More people say they believe in heaven than in hell, and most people who believe in hell think they are not going there. However, Christ is clearly teaching the doctrine of hell in this parable: "And shall cast them into the furnace of fire: there shall be wailing and gnashing of teeth" (v. 50). Here and elsewhere, Christ very graphically describes hell as a place of torment for both body and soul. There will be darkness and fire, suffering and screaming, gnashing of teeth and endless torment.

If you have never before reckoned with this reality of hell, Christ is bringing it before you in this parable. Unless we flee from the wrath to come, it will come upon us without mitigation—forever!

Questions

1. Compare and contrast the first (the sower) and last parable (the net) of this chapter. What do you observe?

2. Mention five points of correspondence between how things work with the dragnet and the kingdom of heaven.

3. This parable mentions the angels. What are some of the other works of angels in the Bible, and what significance does it have that God uses the angels in the judgment?

4. Examine how often and graphically Christ spoke about hell. Why did He do this? How can so many deny or push aside what He taught?

5. Name three comforts you see for believers in this parable.

The Glory of Kingdom Grace:
Some Parables in Luke

The Glory of Kingdom Mercy

THE PARABLE OF THE
GOOD SAMARITAN
(Luke 10:25–37)

And, behold, a certain lawyer...said unto [Jesus],
What is written in the law? how readest thou?
And he answering said, Thou shalt love the Lord
thy God with all thy heart, and with all thy soul,
and with all thy strength, and with all thy mind;
and thy neighbour as thyself. And he said unto
him, Thou hast answered right: this do, and thou
shalt live. But he, willing to justify himself, said
unto Jesus, And who is my neighbour?

—LUKE 10:25–29

9

One of the most well-known of all the parables is what is traditionally called the parable of the good Samaritan. Even many people who do not profess Christianity have heard of it and think of it as a heartwarming story. They are impressed with the caring outsider, who surpassed the "insiders" in tangible love. Some who hold to a social gospel point to this parable as a summary of what they believe. "It's all about making this world a better place," they say. Many believe the moral of the story is simply that we should love others without prejudice and without limit. But when we look at the parable carefully, we see that Christ is describing for us a true heart of mercy.

The Scenery

One day, as Christ was traveling toward Jerusalem to accomplish the purpose for which He had come to this earth (see Luke 9:51), a lawyer emerged from the crowd gathered around Him (v. 25). During this time, lawyers were people who were educated in the law of Moses. They were trained in schools of the rabbis to read and interpret the law of God and apply it to life and society. This lawyer would have been very used to both asking and answering questions. Today, however, he would ask a question of the one of whom the whole roll of the law spoke. And not only that, he would also receive an answer from the one who had the law written upon His heart. We read that he asked Christ this question: "Master, what shall I do to inherit eternal life?" (v. 25).

There is something commendable in the lawyer's question. He clearly realized that this earthly life is not an eternal one. Many today give no thought to anything beyond this life. They are content to live their earthly lives, acquiring all there is to "inherit" now. By contrast, the lawyer's question assumes that this life is not all there is. There is such a thing as *eternal* life.

This lawyer also seemed to realize that eternal life does not simply fall into everyone's lap. Again, many imagine this to be the case. They assume that, with the rare exception, everyone is heading to heaven. They never doubt whether they will have life after death. But this lawyer does not presume like that. His study of the law of Moses has taught him at least two things: there is such a thing as eternal life, and not everyone has it—or a right to it.

When we take a closer look at this lawyer's question, however, we see that there is also something not commendable about it. He asked, "What shall I *do* to inherit eternal life?" (v. 25, emphasis added). He was after an inheritance, and he wanted to know what he needed to *do* to obtain it. You could say that he was ready to climb the ladder of actions, at the top of which he saw an inheritance to be earned. He doesn't even ask, "What *must* I do?" He says, "What *shall* I do?" He was poised, ready and willing to make the climb.

Many people are like this lawyer. They are motivated to go after what they desire and may even have an exemplary self-discipline that pushes them along. Isn't it true, however, that we think of success as going upward? I once read a saying that goes like this: "Many think of this world as a ladder to climb. And so it is. It's a ladder to climb *down*." But this did not seem to enter into the lawyer's mind at all. He aspired to ascend, not descend. By nature this is what we all desire.

Luke tells us two additional things about this lawyer and his motives: he wanted to put Christ to the test (v. 25), all the while justifying himself (v. 29). In other words, he wished to scrutinize Christ's words, all the while shielding himself from any scrutiny. Isn't that a picture of our natural tendency as well, especially as religious people? Instead of justifying *God* and putting ourselves to the test, we are prone to do the exact opposite. We have so much respect for ourselves as law-abiding people.

This becomes especially clear with the lawyer's second question to Jesus: "Who is my neighbour?" (v. 29). He asked this question in a self-justifying way, Luke says (v. 29). He wanted, as it were, to draw a line around those he must love, not holding himself responsible beyond that. We get the idea that the fewer people he needed to consider neighbors, the better. It's as if he were asking, "Whom do *I* have to accept as *my* neighbor? After all, I can't love everyone." He almost seems to be anticipating an answer like this: "Lawyer, that is a brilliant question. There is no way you can worry about loving everyone. We all have our limits."

The Substance

As the searcher of all people's hearts, Christ showed what is fundamentally wrong in this lawyer's religion. He knew nothing of gospel mercy. And Christ could have said this to the man bluntly. But instead, Christ tells this parable to make the lawyer see what he was missing and to show us this truth as well. How does Christ accomplish this through this parable?

First, Christ shows us the ugliness of misery. The lawyer had viewed himself as essentially sinless. He was ready to simply work himself up the ladder of the law into the inheritance that he desired. But Christ's parable brings before him a scene of pitiful misery: "A certain man went down from Jerusalem to Jericho, and fell among thieves, which stripped him of his raiment, and wounded him, and departed, leaving him half dead" (v. 30). Though Augustine famously saw this scene as representing Adam's fall into sin, we don't need to stretch the parable that far to find misery. This scene of the half-dead man points to the reality of sin and all its miserable consequences in this world.

Second, Christ shows us the limits of morality. Contrary to what the lawyer imagines, religion won't make a person inherit eternal life. Think about the priest and Levite, who walk a large circle around this heap of misery, the half-dead man. Especially *they* should have heard the call to act. Aren't the priests to "have compassion on the ignorant, and on them that are out of the way" (Heb. 5:2)? These religious men do not show *mercy*; they show themselves *miserly*. They fail, presumably by asking themselves the kind of question the lawyer did: "And who is my neighbor?"

Third, Christ shows us the beauty of mercy. Christ paints a moving picture. A Samaritan steps onto this scene of misery, and stops, and stoops. Notice that he must have come *down* from the animal's back on which he was riding to help. Christ says, "He had compassion on him" (v. 33). He bound up his "neighbor's" wounds and applied medicine. He lifted him up and transported him to a place of rest and safety. He personally took care of him (v. 34). And when he had to leave, he spent his own money to ensure this man's care. Then he even promised to return and repay any further expenses. Mercy stopped, stooped, and spent.

As beautiful as this portrait is, it would be offensive to the lawyer. Like most of his contemporaries, the lawyer would definitely have excluded a Samaritan from the circle of those whom he considered his neighbors. But it is precisely the Samaritan who displays the fulfillment of the law. Thus Christ puts an irreparable fracture in this man's definition of who his neighbor is. This "non-neighbor" (according to the lawyer's prejudice) is actually the only real neighbor in the story.

The Savior

In this parable, Christ is unveiling Himself in terms of the glory of gospel mercy. It is important to note that the term *mercy*, and words like it, occurs at important places in the gospel according to Luke. Almost every time, it refers to what God does in Jesus Christ. Mary and Zechariah both sang of it in the first chapter of Luke's gospel (vv. 50, 54, 72, 78). The publican in the temple prayed for mercy on the basis of the sacrifice (Luke 18:13). Another occasion is the moving scene, also close to Jericho, when that bundle of misery, blind Bartimaeus, cried out for mercy from the Son of David (Luke 18:35–43). Then Christ, like the Samaritan here, stood still and did all that was required.

In this light, Christ is revealing Himself as the one through whom mercy has come to miserable man. It is as if Christ were saying to the man, "Lawyer, you've asked the right person about eternal life. You have before you not only a prophet who knows your heart and can answer your question perfectly. You also have a priest, who is on His way to display mercy full and free. From heaven He stooped to die for sinners, and on the cross He will spend all that is needed to raise up wounded sinners like you."

The Searchlight

Unfortunately, many think far too narrowly about how this parable applies to them. People commonly speak about being a "good Samaritan." We read of it in our newspapers or hear people talk that way. Someone intervenes heroically in a desperate situation. Perhaps someone is stranded or wounded along the side of the road, and a stranger stops his car to help. Or maybe a car has gone off the side of the road into a swamp, and a passerby jumps in to see if she can help rescue any passengers. Such stories are examples of people displaying courage, bravery, and compassion.

It would be wrong, however, to think that not being this kind of good Samaritan in certain circumstances would be disobedience to Christ's command at the end of this parable. There are times when a person cannot or should not stop to pick up a hitchhiker. If you see a stranded motorist, a cellphone call to a nearby safety patrol station may be all that is necessary and prudent. This parable isn't about the United Nations Children's Fund. Nor is it simply about rehabilitating victims of violence. The application of this parable runs far more deeply and extends far more broadly than engaging in acts for the civic good.

Through this parable Christ is searching out whether our hearts have become centered on mercy. By nature we do not truly reckon with mercy. Granted, our society does talk a lot about compassion. But such compassion can be external and formal, coming from impure motives. People can engage in "compassionate" acts for all sorts of reasons and still not have the heart of mercy, which Christ commends in this parable and elsewhere in His teaching. We all have heard the stereotype of a person who is constantly busy with the needs of strangers around him but neglects the needs of his own wife and children. Such a person should not think that this parable legitimizes what he is doing. Instead, this parable searches us on the following three points:

1. *Have we experienced gospel mercy in Jesus Christ?* As we have seen, the word *mercy* is used most often in the gospel of Luke in connection with Christ and how God deals with sinners through Him. We will never be able to show true mercy to others if we haven't become recipients of God's mercy ourselves. Like the publican in the temple (Luke 18:13), we need to become beggars for God's mercy. We need to lose our "merits" and come to see that we can be saved only out of mercy. Without it, we will never be anything but fallen, lost, and perishing creatures. In the Bible, *mercy* usually refers to God's covenant faithfulness or lovingkindness. It is the tender pity He shows to miserable sinners for His own name's sake. He shows it preeminently in pardoning them and restoring them through the death of His Son. This is the mercy that we need. When we taste it, we say: "Because thy lovingkindness [mercy] is better than life, my lips shall praise thee" (Ps. 63:3). We need to have our minds renewed by the

mercy of God in Christ. We need to have our hearts filled with the mercy of God in Christ. We need to have our hands directed by the mercy of God in Christ.

2. *Have we been made channels of gospel mercy to others?* David, a man who had experienced the mercy of God, asked, "Is there not yet any of the house of Saul, that I may shew the kindness of God unto him?" (2 Sam. 9:3). A man who has truly experienced mercy will be a changed man. If he loves God, whom he has not seen, he will also love his brother, whom he can see (see 1 John 4:20). It's like a torrent of water that comes upon a dry riverbed; that riverbed will help guide the water into low places. So too, the mercy of God comes into the heart of man, which of itself is empty of mercy. That heart then becomes a channel of God's mercy to others, especially those who are poor and needy.

3. *Do we recognize opportunities to display gospel mercy in our everyday lives?* How does this parable play itself out in each of our lives? Like this priest and Levite, we may be returning from public worship, or we may have done our religious exercises for the day. Everything may seem to be going normally and uneventfully. But some evidence of human misery, small or great, confronts us. It isn't just the homeless man sticking halfway out of his cardboard shelter next to the downtown bank building. It isn't just the flyer in your mailbox depicting dying orphans in Africa. It's much more pervasive and demanding than that. It's the church member whom you haven't engaged in meaningful conversation for years. It's your spouse, who is having a difficult day. It's your alcoholic uncle, from whom everyone else keeps their distance. It's someone in tears down the aisle in church. It's someone who has made

it "impossible" for you to forgive him. It's your teenager, who needs you to interrupt your routine to give her a listening ear. It's the neighbor who is irksome to everyone on the street. It's the ailing patient who needs to see your eyes and feel your loving hand as she goes through the valley. It's the student who could use a warm meal between services on the Lord's Day. It's the family that *hasn't* shown up for weeks at church. It's the coworker who seems to *need* so much.

Perhaps you feel the burden of the moment. Perhaps an avalanche of questions fills your mind: "What can I do? What should I do? Can't anyone else do it? Meanwhile, your conscience adds its voice: "If you don't, who will? What if this were you? Aren't you someone who knows the law of God? Didn't you just recite this morning back in 'Jerusalem,' at church or at home, 'Thou shalt love thy neighbor as thyself'"? Now, here's an opportunity to live a mercy-centered life in the everyday.

Somewhere in this array of voices, you close your eyes and wish it were all a dream. You ever so slightly clench your jaw and turn your feet away from the opportunity, and your steps carve out a detour around the opportunity that was there. But this detour is now carved into the fabric of history, and the memory of that missed opportunity springs like an arrow out of the bow right into your conscience and says, "This man's religion is vain" (James 1:26).

The only true way to become a fountain of mercy to others is to experience infinite mercy yourself. When God stoops down in Jesus Christ to pour out His mercy in your soul, that mercy becomes a fountain in you. Though something in you may still make you want to walk away from the misery that you see, the love of Christ ultimately constrains you. Your spouse, your children, your coworkers, your fellow church members, and people all around you will taste the mercy of God as it is channeled through you.

Questions

1. Do you recognize mercy in the way Christ deals with the lawyer? If you do, how do you see Christ showing mercy?

2. Define *mercy*. Why is it easy to be religious and yet not merciful?

3. What does this parable have to do with social justice and works of relief in the world? Is it possible still to have a religion like the priest and the Levite while being busy with such things?

4. Give four scenarios from your everyday life (e.g., from recent weeks) in which the call of mercy came to you. Think through what a response of mercy would have looked like. How about an unmerciful response?

5. Why is it that true Christians, who have experienced God's mercy, often fail to be channels of mercy? What must we do so that we follow the call of mercy in a fresh and vibrant way?

The Glory of Kingdom Fruitfulness

THE PARABLE OF THE UNFRUITFUL FIG TREE
(Luke 13:1–9)

There were present at that season some that told him of the Galilaeans, whose blood Pilate had mingled with their sacrifices. And Jesus answering said unto them, Suppose ye that these Galilaeans were sinners above all the Galilaeans, because they suffered such things? I tell you, Nay: but, except ye repent, ye shall all likewise perish.

—LUKE 13:1–3

10

One day in the early spring some years ago, I saw a dogwood splendidly in bloom. I commented on its beauty to the owner of the tree, who stood nearby. "This is the first year it has bloomed like this," he said. "In fact, in previous years, it was doing miserably. I thought I should just take it down and replace it with another." His explanation begged a question, which he proceeded to answer. "I was complaining about the tree to a farmer, who said, 'Try giving it a few kicks.'" He paused: "I don't know the scientific explanation, but last fall I kicked it firmly a few times, and look at the results."

There is an interesting spiritual lesson here. Often, blows to the trunk of our life help us grow spiritually. Hardship can be helpful. Yet the Lord does more than that in His people's lives. In this parable, usually known as the unfruitful fig tree, Christ tells us that He both *digs* around us and *fertilizes* us (Luke 13:8) in order that we would bring forth fruit.

The Scenery

This parable has an interesting context. The first verse of the chapter mentions a horrifying atrocity that Pilate ordered. Bloodshed was not uncommon in the many conflicts between the Romans and Jews during this time. However, this time human blood had become mingled with the blood of animals that were being sacrificed daily at the massive temple complex in Jerusalem (v. 1). This would have been appalling even to pagans, and much more so to the Jews. The temple would have been desecrated in a horrible way. And if the temple was not the boast of their nation and religion, what was?

The people clearly wanted some reassurance from Christ that they were different from and better than the victims of the calamities around them. That way they could put up a barrier between themselves and the real message of the calamity. Christ's response shows this: "Suppose ye that these Galilaeans were sinners above all the Galilaeans, because they suffered such things?" (v. 2). These people wanted to rank themselves on a higher plane than the victims. If they couldn't do that, they would have to face the fact that such judgment could just as easily have come upon them, and would, if things didn't change. Would Christ help reassure them? Would He, in the words of one of the prophets, "heal the wound of my people lightly" (Jer. 8:11)?

The Substance

At first glance, the parable might seem to have little or nothing to do with calamity. Nevertheless, the context suggests that it does, and a careful reading proves it. Here is how the parable unfolds. Christ pictures a fig tree in the midst of a vineyard. For three years, the owner came looking for and expecting fruit from the tree, but did not find any. So he instructed the keeper of the vineyard to cut it down. "Why cumbereth it the ground?" (13:7). In contemporary terms, we would say, "It is wasting space, soil, water, and care that could otherwise be put to better use." Then Christ records the plea of the laborer to the owner: "Lord, let it alone this year also, till I shall dig about it, and dung it: and if it bear fruit, well: and if not, then after that thou shalt cut it down" (vv. 8–9).

Christ announced the theme of the parable already in verse 3: "Except ye repent, ye shall all likewise perish." The parable only serves to drive home this point (vv. 6–9). The basic message is this: "God is still giving you time and means to repent and bring forth fruits of repentance; if not, you too will soon be cut down."

National calamities are messages to nations as well as to individuals. Though the parable can be applied to individuals, Christ was very likely also referring to the nation of Israel's unfruitfulness. The parable speaks of a *fig tree* in a *vineyard*—a unique plant in such surroundings. Israel was a unique nation— one set apart from the surrounding nations. Thus it was to bring forth a unique fruit. All nations rise and fall according to God's plan, with God giving each of them an appointed time and purpose. God bears with nations, but He also judges them.

The Savior

Christ unveils His glory in this parable in terms of gospel fruitfulness. His portrait can easily be seen in the vinedresser of the passage. The "digging" and "fertilizing" (v. 8) in the parable have spiritual parallels. When a farmer digs around a tree, he is aerating the soil and loosening the encrusted earth, which is unsettling for the tree. Yet, ultimately, the tree can be enriched by it, especially if it helps the fertilizer to drop down into the roots. So too, afflictions can shake up and unsettle us; however, because of Jesus Christ, God's grace thus reaches the roots of our lives and produces fruit. The

Lord digs around our lives by the work of His Holy Spirit. He sends vital nutrients through His Spirit from His cross.

In light of the rest of the gospel, believers recognize that Christ's death and resurrection specifically is the reason His people are able to bear fruit. He bore the punishment due to His people for their unfruitfulness and in turn became the source for all their fruit-bearing. On the cross, He interceded for transgressors, that they would be given a space of time for repentance (Luke 23:34). In that way, we can all rightly say that we are living on borrowed time.

The Searchlight

Terrorists captured the whole world's attention when they brought down the Twin Towers in New York on September 11, 2001. All people seemed to talk about for weeks was the number of people who died, the rescue efforts and rescuers, the perpetrators of the crime, the stories of survival, the political tensions, and how to prevent such a thing again. Man wants to bring all his available wisdom to bear on a situation like this and feels the need to speak and act. But it is even more important that we *listen* at times like this.

This is not true only of disasters on a large scale, like terrorist attacks, earthquakes, or tsunamis. It is also true when difficulties strike in our communities, families, or our own lives. Calamities are reminders that God has put us on His earth, and He can take any of us away at any time. We have not been made only to breathe God's air, eat God's food, and drink God's water. We have been placed on earth for the purpose of bringing forth fruit to God. The basic question is this: Have we yielded the fruit that we were intended to yield?

The first great fruit, which brings forth all others, is the fruit of true repentance and faith (13:3, 5). Often, we don't think of repentance as fruit. Yet John the Baptist had already called for the "fruits worthy of repentance" (Luke 3:8). The Reformers often spoke of the whole Christian life under the heading of "repentance." Psalm 51:17 says, "The sacrifices of God are a broken spirit: a broken and a contrite heart, O God, thou wilt not despise." If even calamities would bring us to offer true heart-sacrifices unto our great owner, He would have His fruit.

Questions

1. We may or may not think of others as worse sinners than we are; however, we all have ways of distancing ourselves from the message God sends us through calamities. What are some ways we do that?

2. What is a calamity that you and your nation have recently faced or are facing now? How does the parable shed light on your circumstances?

3. Think about what it means to "cumber the ground." How do we do this? What insight does this give into the life that God rightly demands from us?

4. Read Hosea 14:4–7. In what way could this passage be seen as a positive ending to this parable?

5. How does God "dig" and "dung" the lives of His people? Give examples from the Scriptures of how God did this in certain people's experience.

6. Explain how repentance is fruit. Luther says that "the whole of the Christian life is repentance." Do you agree or disagree with him, and why?

The Glory of Kingdom Wisdom

THE PARABLE OF THE RICH FOOL
(Luke 12:13–21)

But God said unto him, Thou fool, this night thy soul shall be required of thee: then whose shall those things be, which thou hast provided? So is he that layeth up treasure for himself, and is not rich toward God.

—LUKE 12:20–21

11

When I lived in the Middle East for about a year, I quickly learned that even today, money changers are powerful people. Down the street from where I lived was a small but busy place where lots of money changed hands. I quickly learned that American currency was esteemed more highly than any other kind. The owners didn't care for our country, but they loved our currency. They might refuse to trade currencies of nations in fiscal or political crisis or devalue those currencies, but this was not the case with the American dollar. It was readily accepted, even on the other side of the world.

Heaven, however, doesn't accept any currency other than its own. The man with the biggest bank account on earth is as poor as the man in jail with the biggest debt, if neither has the right spiritual currency. Instead, Christ tells us we must be "rich toward God" (Luke 12:21).

The Scenery

When Christ came to earth to live among men, He came to a world filled with greed—and this greed evidenced itself in conflicts and disputes over resources similar to those we hear about today. As He taught the people about God and their souls and how to live in this world, Christ stressed the need to live in dependence on God (Luke 12:1–12). He reminded them that God takes care of all those who love and fear Him. If God does not forget the sparrows, would He forget His disciples (v. 6)? He wouldn't forget them in the needs of their daily lives, nor would He leave them in more dire situations. If, for example, they would have to appear before magistrates, God would give His Holy Spirit to help them say what they needed to say.

This promise of help for those who would appear before magistrates triggers a thought in someone in the crowd. This man had a dispute with his brother. He got the idea that Christ might be able to help him in this situation. Perhaps Christ would take his side, and his brother would have to give up the part of the inheritance he was claiming as his own. And so he blurted out, "Master, speak to my brother, that he divide the inheritance with me" (v. 13).

The man had not truly understood a word of what Christ was saying. True, he was listening to Christ, but ultimately he had no spiritual need for Him. He needed His help only with the financial conflict in which he was involved. In this, he is like so many so-called Christians who hope that their Christianity will be able to help them get ahead in life.

With perfect wisdom, Christ refused this man's request. Why did He do this? For Him, acceding to this man's request would be departing from His Father's appointment. He was not sent to solve earthly disputes. He did give spiritual and practical principles by which men should live, including guidance for those who have something against their brother (Matt. 18:15–20). He would also send His Spirit to enable His people to live in harmony (Acts 2:42). And yet the Father had not appointed Him as an earthly judge in a Jewish court.

Moreover, the man's question showed a disposition, or heart attitude, that was the opposite of dependence on God. He might have appeared to be depending on Christ by coming to Him with this request, but Christ was just a means to an end for him. His inheritance was his goal and idol, and, ironically, he felt he needed Christ to get his idol back into his possession.

The Substance

By way of this parable, Christ poignantly taught the folly of a life lived for earthly goods. To illustrate His warning against covetousness in verse 15, Christ first described the kind of person this world highly esteems. It's someone who has assets (land), receives good profits (harvests), and acts with business savvy (planning to build bigger barns). His investment strategy would enable him to grow wealthier and wealthier. Note that, as far as we can tell, this man did not acquire his goods through any wrongdoing. There was nothing corrupt or illegal about his gains in wealth, except, of course, that he appeared ungrateful and did not distribute to the poor.

Though there may have been no crime against human laws in this rich fool's conduct, there was a spiritual crime of the highest sort. Christ pinpointed it forcibly in verse 21. This man's identity and plan for his life were wrapped up in his possessions.

It's interesting to notice that the rich fool addressed his soul (v. 19). This man was not unaware that he had a soul. He even spoke to his soul, something from which even Christians can learn a lesson (see Pss. 42:5, 11; 103:1). But the catastrophic problem with that address was that he comforted his soul with stuff (v. 19a). He placated his soul with pleasantries (v. 19b).

How dreadful then is God's sentence in verse 20: "Thou fool, this night thy soul shall be required of thee: then whose shall those things be which thou hast provided?" Whereas this man was feeding his soul with stuff, God, who created every soul, in one moment disconnected this man's soul from his body and from all his goods. We see, as it were, this man's poor soul travel in an instant from his farm, crops, land, and life into an eternity, where none of his riches could help him at all. With all his business savvy, he had never learned the first lesson of life: "You have a soul that can never die."

The Savior

Christ here unveils His glory in terms of gospel wisdom. We see Christ in terms of the one who uncovers the lack of gospel wisdom. The man of this passage wanted Christ to fill his wallet and give him his just due. When you read that, you can't help but think of the prodigal son, who said something very similar: "Father, give me the portion of goods that falleth to me" (Luke 15:12). How blessed it is when Christ uncovers us to the valuelessness of accumulating the things of this world, in light of eternity. Our earthly currency will be useless there. Christ pointed the man in the direction he needed to go. He needed to become rich toward God (Luke 12:21).

We see Christ also as the precise embodiment of what gospel wisdom looks like. The miracle of the gospel is that God's riches come to needy sinners who look to Him for them. They come at Christ's expense. This redemption is not corruptible like gold and silver. It is even more precious. It has been bought at the price of the precious blood of Christ (1 Peter 1:19). At the cross Christ paid the price for sinners like this covetous man, in order that they may have an inheritance that fades not away, reserved in heaven for those who believe.

The Searchlight

The glory of Christ as it shines in this parable uncovers how our lives are so easily bound up with material possessions, which we have neither brought into the world, nor will take from the world (1 Tim. 6:7). This was exactly the problem with Christ's questioner (v. 13) and all natural people as they are born in this world. We live for things and get our identity from them. We measure ourselves by our portfolios and our ability to acquire things this year that might have been beyond us last year. This is not true only of unconverted people; God's children struggle with covetousness as well. So often they find themselves too attached to the things of this world. How we need the Holy Spirit to convince us again and again that we cannot feed our souls with stuff. It cannot and will not satisfy!

On the other hand, the parable sheds light upon our path in order that we by faith might live lives of gospel wisdom. This parable is a call to all of us: "Wherefore do ye spend money for that which is not bread? and your labour for that which satisfieth not? hearken diligently unto me, and eat ye that which is good, and let your soul delight itself in fatness" (Isa. 55:2). God's grace in Jesus Christ is what will truly satisfy...and make us "rich toward God" (Luke 12:21).

Questions

1. Define *covetousness* (v. 15). What are some signs of covetousness becoming pervasive in a church? How can a church diagnose and turn back covetousness?

2. When is it wrong to "build bigger barns," and when is it not?

3. The Puritans had a quaint expression: "sitting loose from this world's goods." Compare this expression with Luke 12:15 and discuss ways in which you reinforce that posture toward material goods.

4. Before God, the questioner (v. 13) was really no different from his brother. How does the parable prove that point? Is it true that mere poverty itself is no better than mere riches?

5. How should this rich man have talked to his soul, and what should he have said (see v. 19)? For help, compare Revelation 3:17–18.

6. Look up Ephesians 1:7, 18; 2:7; 4:8; and Colossians 1:27 and 2:2, and discuss the relevance of these verses as you compare them to Luke 12:21.

The Glory of Kingdom Provision

THE PARABLE OF THE GREAT SUPPER
(Luke 14:12–24)

But when thou makest a feast, call the poor, the maimed, the lame, the blind: and thou shalt be blessed; for they cannot recompense thee: for thou shalt be recompensed at the resurrection of the just.

—LUKE 14:13–14

~ *12* ~

Why do many who seem so close to the kingdom of God still end up perishing? This is one of the most perplexing questions we might try to wrap our minds around. Of course, the Bible teaches us the doctrines that help us to understand this, such as the fundamental truths of election and reprobation and the total inability of man, whose evil heart will not and cannot believe in its own strength. These truths give us the deepest answers to this question. In the parable of the great supper in Luke 14, Christ also sheds light on this question in a very pointed way.

The Scenery

Christ was at the home of a Pharisee to eat bread on the Sabbath day (v. 1). He used the occasion to teach those with Him at the meal about offering and receiving hospitality. When others invite us, we should have a humble spirit and choose a lowly place to sit, rather than thinking we deserve the best place (vv. 7–11). In regard to offering hospitality, we should also have a gracious attitude, welcoming strangers and others who are not able to reward us in return (vv. 13–14).

Perhaps because Christ's teaching went so directly against the grain of what the Pharisees were used to, one man wanted to change the subject. At first glance, it seemed

that he switched to a more "spiritual" topic. He said, "Blessed
is he that shall eat bread in the kingdom of God" (v. 15).
These words are true and wonderful in and of themselves.
However, you get the definite impression from the context
that the man was using this statement to escape the force
of what Christ was teaching. It allowed him and the other
guests to turn away from Christ's direct words to a less objec-
tionable truth—or so he may have thought. We shouldn't be
surprised when people use truth this way. Perhaps it happens
most among religious people, like those in whose company
Christ was just now. Or perhaps this man wanted to sound
more pious than Christ. Maybe he thought something like
this: "Let Jesus dwell on a mundane topic like hospitality. I
will talk about truly worthwhile things—like the feast in the
kingdom of God."

In response to this man's comment, Christ told a parable using the scenery of a great supper. The Bible frequently
uses the picture of a feast to symbolize the joy and provision
that gospel salvation affords (e.g., Ps. 23:5–6; Isa. 25:6; Rev.
3:20). The point Christ makes in this parable will uncover
the hypocrisy of both this man and many others who think
themselves religious.

The Substance

Many people undoubtedly thought this man was already part
of the kingdom of God—and he probably thought so himself. But Christ's parable makes clear that belonging to the
kingdom involves much more than saying nice things about
it. Behind lofty and pious-sounding thoughts may be hearts
that are still completely lost.

The parable also clears God from all wrongdoing when it comes to man's perdition. Instead, the fault rests with man, who indifferently fails to comply with God's invitation in the gospel. Note the following three aspects:

1. *God has furnished a complete salvation.* There are a number of features of this supper that illustrate particular aspects of the salvation God has wrought in the gospel. Notice that this supper is not a potluck, to which everyone is asked to bring a dish. Instead, a certain host takes the initiative and single-handedly prepares the meal. This is exactly what God does in salvation. He is the one who initiates and provides. Moreover, notice that the supper is a great supper where all things are ready (v. 17). It is a not a small meal that only a handful of people can enjoy or that requires the guests' help to make it adequate. Likewise, God's salvation is a great salvation, and it is sufficient for many. Sinners do not ultimately perish because there is no great salvation to be found.

2. *God invites in the gospel.* Those who were not at this supper could not say that they weren't invited. In fact, the host seemed to have invited those who refused *sooner* and *more specifically* than the others. He had invited them beforehand, and on the day that everything was ready, he sent a servant specifically to tell them so (v. 17). By the end of the parable, the invitation had been extended to basically anyone who could be found. Likewise, the gospel invitation is broad and free. Anyone who hungers and thirsts is invited to come to Christ for spiritual food and drink.

3. *Even the unworthy are invited.* This gospel feast is so very different from the feasts we are used to having. No one is disqualified because of unworthiness, disability, or

distance; the second half of the parable (vv. 21–24) makes that clear. No one could say that he was unworthy to come because he was blind or lame. And no one was too out of the way or too far away to reach. No one could say that the host's servant passed him over because he was hidden in the byways or hedges.

Some years back, a friend said something to me that I will never forget. It was simple and yet so profound. He said, "The reason people don't do what they are supposed to do is because they want to do something else." It is not only true in everyday life; it is especially true spiritually. The substance of this parable is that man, even religious man, is indifferent to the sincere and well-meant invitations of the gospel. Christ pinpoints this indifference with one short sentence: "They all with one consent began to make excuse" (v. 18). They esteemed God's salvation as *less* than the things that the world and their own sinful hearts settled on for significance.

The Savior

Christ unveils His glory in this parable in terms of gospel provision. When we look at this parable in the light of Christ's ministry to publicans and sinners, as well as to the lame and blind and other social outcasts of His time, we recognize that Christ can be seen at many points in this parable. We see that Christ's gracious coming proclaims the arrival of gospel provision. There would be no feast apart from His mediatorial work, which can bring fallen man back into fellowship with God. Through Him, the gospel table can be furnished with rich provisions, even spiritual blessings in high places. His death has brought in pardon and acceptance with God; His resurrection has sealed an everlasting righteousness. Eternal life, joy, and fellowship are all blessings flowing from His cross and resurrection. He Himself embodies the blessings of salvation for His people. He feeds His people with Himself. He satisfies their spiritual hunger and thirst. He brings His people together around a table at which He is the host, the bread, the water, and the life.

We also see that the Pharisees and others who made excuses not to partake of gospel provision rejected Christ. The people making excuses were ultimately dishonoring the host. They were so bent on rejecting the supper and the host that they sent Christ to the cross, demonstrating how deep their rejection of the host went.

Finally, we see that Christ's work is the basis on which God graciously calls men, women, and children—no matter how great their sin—back to Himself. Through His ministry Christ was calling fallen sinners back to Himself, and now that He is exalted, He still calls through the gospel ministry. He calls His servants to reason with men, seeking to persuade them with every possible argument to lay aside their indifference and come to the banquet supper of God. By His Holy Spirit, He seeks out those hidden away in the highways and byways of sin and draws them savingly and effectually to fellowship with the triune God.

The Searchlight

Indifference to gospel provisions takes on different forms and differing degrees of vehemence. As we trace the three excuses as they are given in the parable, a searchlight shines on our hearts. Do we have the same indifference to the gospel call? Let's look at each excuse briefly in turn.

The first excuse is this: "I have bought a piece of ground, and I must needs go and see it: I pray thee have me excused" (v. 18). This excuse is more politely worded than the others. The man asked to be excused and seemed to want the host to understand that he would have come if he could have. But beneath this politeness was an attitude of indifference. This man made it clear that his plot of land was more interesting to him than the feast.

The second man is less courteous. He simply said that he intends to try out his oxen. He clearly was so engrossed in his possessions and work that he had no time even to reason his way out of this invitation. He expected the host to understand the validity of his excuse.

But the third man's excuse was the harshest. He implied that the host had invited him at an inconvenient time. He had just married, so the host could not possibly expect him to consider seriously this invitation.

Are we indifferent to the gospel? Or are our lives marked by an eagerness to comply with the Lord's invitations? Do earthly duties, privileges, and pleasures take second place to the glorious spiritual banquet that God has furnished in Jesus Christ? Is our response politely pushing the host away? Is our response perhaps more brazen even than that, suggesting that the Lord surely can't expect us to leave such things as our possessions and pleasures for His banquet? What language do our actions speak? Let us take stock. Anything less than full, eager compliance with the gospel is nothing less than indifference toward the host, who has freely furnished a great feast and freely invites men into fellowship with Himself.

Notice that it isn't enough to know about the supper or to be invited to the supper. It isn't even enough to respond to the invitation. Nothing less than coming to the gospel supper by faith is adequate. This is what Christ is preaching through this parable. We cannot plead our unworthiness or say that somehow we don't measure up to the feast. The presence of the many maimed and blind at the feast makes invalid any such excuse we give to the Lord. Let's take heed to the admonition: "Let us labour therefore to enter into that rest, lest any man fall after the same example of unbelief" (Heb. 4:11).

Questions

1. Why does Christ compare salvation to a supper or feast?

2. How does God invite people to come to the gospel? Can anyone say, "I have never been truly invited?"

3. What sorts of excuses do we use, or have you heard, for not believing the gospel? What are modern-day equivalents for the oxen the second man had just purchased?

4. Why do people's excuses sometimes sound more plausible than they really are? How can they sound pious?

5. How can people be "compelled" to come in (v. 23)?

The Glory of Kingdom Love

THE PARABLE OF THE PRODIGAL SON
(Luke 15)

And the son said unto him, Father, I have sinned against heaven, and in thy sight, and am no more worthy to be called thy son. But the father said to his servants, Bring forth the best robe, and put it on him; and put a ring on his hand, and shoes on his feet: and bring hither the fatted calf, and kill it; and let us eat, and be merry: For this my son was dead, and is alive again; he was lost, and is found.

—LUKE 15:20–24

13

The parable of the prodigal son is probably the best known of all Christ's parables. It offers not only a gripping story but also a beautiful summary of the gospel of God's love and forgiveness. Though this parable is essentially about true repentance (vv. 7, 10, 18, 21), it does more than simply illustrate and apply the doctrine of repentance. Though it does that stunningly and memorably, this parable actually gives us a way to view the work of grace *from the perspective of the heart of the Father.*

The Scenery

The scene is not difficult to picture. Despite a few references that would fit the ancient Jewish setting better than our own (servants, the shame of pig farming, a fatted calf), everything else seems universal and familiar. However, there are a number of important cues in the chapter that we should not miss.

One cue we need to notice is the *form* of the parable. We are used to seeing three parables in this chapter, namely, the parables of the lost sheep, the lost coin, and the lost sons. However, according to verse 3, we should instead think of this account as one long parable with three parts. These three parts move in a spiral-like motion, culminating in the story of the two lost sons. It's as if Christ were saying, "Think of the care and diligence of a shepherd who seeks a lost sheep, or a woman looking for a lost silver coin. Think of the joy they both feel when they find what they had lost. Now think of a father who has lost his son…."

We also need to notice the *occasion* for the parable (vv. 2–3). In His travels toward Jerusalem, Christ had made Himself approachable to publicans and sinners (Luke 15:1–2), much to the evident chagrin of the Pharisees. They complain, "This man receiveth sinners, and eateth with them" (v. 2). As true and glorious as this statement is, they utter it as a complaint! It's sobering to think that it is possible to *complain about the gospel*, but that is essentially what was happening here.

Finally, we need to notice *the vantage point* of the parable. This parable is Christ's answer to the Pharisees' bitter complaint. We could think of it this way: Much like the father in the parable who "came out, and intreated" the elder brother (v. 28), so too Christ left the company of these repenting sinners to entreat the Pharisees through this parable. This then is Christ's entreaty to gospel complainers.

The Substance

There are three main elements to the message of this parable. First, Christ is showing our departure from God. Man has departed from God, and he is now lost, cut off, and alienated from fellowship with Him. Like the lost sheep, he has lost the nearness of the shepherd, and thus also his nurture, protection, and leading. Ultimately, he has lost life itself. Like the lost coin, the sinner may have the image of his Maker stamped upon him, but he is now lost and unusable until he is found. Like the younger son, the sinner has preferred the far country of his own desires to the presence of God. In the presence of God are light and life, and in the far country are darkness and death. The elder son is no less cut off from the father. Though he may be in geographical proximity to him, his heart prefers his friends over his father. The fact that he slaves away in his father's house really means nothing about his allegiance. Clearly, both sons are cut off from the true source of life and pine away in their self-chosen death, one in a swine trough, the other in the trap of a self-righteous jealousy and bitterness.

Yet this does not exhaust the brilliance of the parable as it describes our departure from God. For the parable goes on to consider the sinner as lost—from God's perspective. Here lies the real power of the parable. Notice how Christ spends little time on the sheep's experience of being lost, but rather focuses on the shepherd having lost the sheep. Christ spends no time on the dynamic of the coin being out of circulation, hidden away in the dark, but focuses instead on the woman missing the coin and her diligent search for it. In the parable of the two sons, Christ does spend some time describing what it looks like for both these sons to be lost. But He twice points us to the father and lingers, as it were, over what this lostness entailed for him. He has the father repeat twice, "This my son was dead, and is alive again; he was lost, and is found (vv. 24, 32). The point is this: that which is lost is not just lost by itself; it is lost *from God's perspective.*

Second, the parable shows God's recovery of the sinner. In the parable, the prodigal did not immediately return to his father when the famine first arose or when he had run out of the goods he had. The prodigal still had some options—at least, so he thought. He joined himself to a citizen of that far country. The word *join* in the original means that he "glued" or "cemented" himself to this man. He essentially engaged himself in covenant with this man, placing himself under this man's authority. This was not an advantageous position, for we read that "no man gave unto him" (v. 16). All of this illustrates the fact that the prodigal *could not* and *would not* recover himself. He would only further enslave himself, until "he came to himself" (v. 17). A critical change took place when his right mind returned to him (compare Mark 5:15). Then he began to reckon with "heaven" (v. 18) or, more precisely, the God of heaven. He also came to see himself, his misery, and sin. He said, "I perish with hunger" (v. 17). This word in the original literally means "I am destroying myself." He had come to see the death into which he had cast himself. Finally, he also received a changed view of his father (see v. 17).

What is important to see, however, is that God's love was pursuing this lost sinner. This change of his mind was the *result of*, not the *reason for*, free grace. Twice the father said that his son "was dead, and is alive again; he was lost, and is found" (vv. 24, 32). Christ stresses that he "was found." After all, what can a dead sinner do for his recovery? Just like a lost sheep needs a shepherd to find it and a lost coin needs a woman to find it, so too the prodigal son needs his father to find him. Likewise, a dead sinner needs God in Christ to find him. That is exactly what was happening with Christ and these publicans and sinners (Luke 15:1–2).

Third, the parable teaches the sinner's rejoicing in God. It is important to notice that, in the parable, joy had its origin in the father's love. The son was still thinking of ways he might become his father's servant when the father's love sent him running out to his son. When they met, the father's love drove away the spirit of bondage under which the son was suffering. The parable pictures it this way: "His father saw him, and had compassion, and ran, and fell on his neck, and kissed him" (v. 20). What joy must have filled the son's heart! The spiritual truth is clear. When the Lord seeks, finds, and recovers a lost sinner, He pours out His love into the sinner's heart (see Rom. 5:5). As a result, there comes "joy in God through our Lord Jesus Christ" (Rom. 5:11).

The Savior

In this parable, Christ unveils Himself in relationship to gospel love. That many have found it difficult to see Christ in this parable demonstrates that He is veiling Himself. When people read about the prodigal's father, they immediately think of the Father in the Godhead. It is important to remember, however, that the Father reveals Himself through the Son; the Son's words and deeds all speak of His Father. For that reason, Christ says elsewhere to Philip, "Have I been so long time with you, and yet hast thou not known me, Philip? He that hath seen me hath seen the Father; and how sayest thou then, Show us the Father?" (John 14:9). The point, then, is that the father of the parable shows us the *seeking, securing,* and *saving* love shown by God in Jesus Christ to lost sinners like the publicans (see Luke 15:1–2). Let's look at each of these three aspects briefly:

1. *In Christ we see the seeking love of God.* Just as the shepherd seeks the lost sheep and the woman the lost coin, so too, in Christ, God is seeking lost sinners, whether they are lost

in misery, like the younger son, or lost in self-righteousness, like the older son. Just as the publicans of this passage were surprised by the seeking grace of Christ, so too our hearts should be broken by the love that God displays in the gospel of Christ. Through the power of Christ's Holy Spirit we, like this prodigal, should "come to our senses" and acknowledge our sin against God.

2. *In Christ we see the securing love of God.* Christ not only sought sinners, but He bought them. His whole mission was to ransom them. On the cross, He was cast *out of* the Father's house to take the reproach of prodigals upon Himself, allowing them to return *to* the Father's house. He was willing to take the sin and shame and the reproach and wretchedness of sinners upon Himself to give them instead acceptance, pardon, and the garments of salvation.

3. *In Christ we see the saving love of God.* Later on, when Zacchaeus was welcomed back as a "son of Abraham" (Luke 19:9), Christ would say concerning Himself, "The Son of man is come to seek and to save that which was lost" (Luke 19:10). We could say that the prodigal was brought into the experience of salvation by that same saving grace. Because of Christ, God can accept sinners and bring them into fellowship with Himself. For Christ's sake, they can be restored as sons of God. And instead of being dead, they are made alive in Christ!

The Searchlight

Are we dead or alive? Lost or found? The answer to these questions depends on our relationship to God in Christ, symbolized by the father in this parable. If we are still removed from Him by our sin and fall, as we all are by nature, we are lost. We will remain lost until we come to our senses and return to God.

Those who do not believe they are lost but do not know and share in the joy of lost sinners being saved should be convicted by this parable. Christ received sinners and ate with them (Luke 15:2). But the Pharisees refused to partake in the joy and celebration, thereby condemning themselves as being without love and life. If we know grace, we will have a gracious spirit toward the lost. Grace and joy are "close cousins," you might say. Where the one is, the other will not be far behind.

This does not mean that everyone can always discern the beginnings of new life equally well. For example, when Saul of Tarsus was saved, some in Jerusalem "believed not that he was a disciple" (Acts 9:26). This still can happen today. And yet this is different from the anger of the elder brother. The elder brother was still in the bondage of the covenant of works, and he was envious and vexed that his brother was not suffering as he was. Let the conversion of sinners around us be a test of whether we have truly tasted that the Lord is gracious, or whether we perhaps are still operating under a legalistic scheme that rejoices only when others are in the same or even greater bondage than we are. How necessary it is, for a first time or afresh, that God's grace in Jesus Christ bring us into the truth and experience of salvation and to "joy in God through our Lord Jesus Christ, by whom we have now received the atonement" (Rom. 5:11).

Questions

1. Reflect on this "mighty famine" (Luke 15:14). Humanly speaking, if this famine had never come, the prodigal would never have been converted. What other "mighty" things can God use, besides famines, to stop us in our self-seeking lives? Why do the things we most resist often prove to be the best for us?

2. Is it possible to come to Christ without a sense, however small, of His mercy? Consider your answer by consulting other Scripture passages in the Old and New Testament that describe people coming to the Lord.

3. Is it true that conversion involves only a few small changes, mostly unseen? Trace the events of verses 17–19 and notice how many things turn upside down for the prodigal once he comes to himself. What does this teach us about the depth of our fall and the need for the initial and sustained renewal of our minds (Rom. 12:1–2)?

4. What does it mean that "when he was yet a great way off, his father saw him" (v. 20)? Think of other passages in which God sees a sinner in his need and misery.

5. Why doesn't the parable tell us how the elder brother responded to the father? What responses are possible? How does the work of the Holy Spirit fit into this?

The Glory of Kingdom Prudence

THE PARABLE OF THE
UNJUST STEWARD
(Luke 16:1–18)

He that is faithful in that which is least is faithful also in much: and he that is unjust in the least is unjust also in much. If therefore ye have not been faithful in the unrighteous mammon, who will commit to your trust the true riches?

—LUKE 16:10–11

14

In the news, we frequently read about financial scandals of one kind or another. People in positions of power, including CEOs, mismanage funds and assets and sometimes bring about the collapse of whole companies. The effects of such scandals have ripple effects at home and abroad. Sadly, through these kinds of events, expressions like "loan sharks" and "writing off debt" have become household terms. But the mismanagement of money is not a new phenomenon. It happened in biblical times as well, and, in this parable, usually known as the parable of the unjust steward, Christ uses a case of financial mismanagement to illustrate and drive home important gospel lessons.

The Scenery

The story line of the parable is relatively simple: a rich man had a steward managing the affairs of his estate. This particular steward was used to operating with large amounts of resources. For example, one hundred measures of oil (v. 6) would have amounted to eight hundred or nine hundred gallons, the equivalent of three years of wages for an average breadwinner. Likewise, a hundred measures of wheat (v. 7) was equivalent to about eleven hundred bushels and about seven and a half years of labor. So, clearly, this steward was comfortable around things worth quite a bit of money—as it turned out, too comfortable. While he was around such vast resources day in and day out, his sinful heart drew him into a pattern of mismanagement (v. 2). He should have served his master faithfully, but the allure of the wealth that slid through his fingers actually became too strong for him. To our sinful hearts, money has a powerful attraction. That's why Christ referred to money as unrighteous mammon (v. 9). Mammon was the false god of money, wealth, and greed. Since none of us can serve two masters (Matt. 6:24), the point quickly came when this steward switched his allegiance from his master to this mammon.

The Substance

Christ is making three distinct points in this parable. The first is about covetousness. When we are covetous, we desire things apart from God and in the place of God. That was the root of this unjust steward's undoing. Let's not think religious people cannot be covetous. In fact, this passage tells us that the Pharisees scoffed at the parable upon hearing it because they themselves were "covetous" (v. 14). Thus they conveniently dismissed what Christ was seeking to expose in them.

Many have been confused by verse 9. Christ says, "Make yourselves friends of the mammon of unrighteousness: that, when ye fail, they may receive you into everlasting habitations." I believe what Christ is saying is this: "Even though many use money wickedly and even worship it as a god, My disciples ought to use money in a way that promotes true and lasting friendship in and through Jesus Christ." How many faithful Christians do not heed this command of Christ by giving tangible support to ministry and missionary causes? Through these means, blessed by God, sinners come to know Christ, the "friend of publicans and sinners" (Matt. 11:19). These everlasting habitations of which Christ speaks refer to the mansions Christ is preparing for His people. There the whole company of the faithful will join together in blessing God from whom all blessings ultimately come. Calvin put it like this: "We should deal humanely and benevolently with our neighbors, that when we come to the tribunal of God the fruit of our liberality may return to us."

The second point Christ makes is that of gospel prudence. We don't know how long the steward mismanaged his master's estate, but at some point, word reached the master, and charges were made. The man realized that his days of employment were numbered, and he began to reflect on what he should do. He knew his situation was desperate. He decided in these last days or hours of his stewardship to ingratiate himself to some of his master's debtors by reducing their debts (v. 4). It is debated whether he was permitted to do this, but it's clear that he took advantage of the opportunity to do so. This apparently did not escape the notice of the master. Surprisingly, the master told him that "he had done wisely" (v. 8).

Notice that Christ is not condoning what the steward did as *proper*. But He is clearly saying that it was *prudent*. It was realistic foresight and ingenuity that prompted the man to find a way of escape for himself from his desperate predicament. It was something like what the prodigal son did in the pigsty. He too was in desperate need and took action to remedy it. And isn't this what the publicans and sinners who heard Christ were doing? They had mismanaged their lives terribly and were in a desperate condition. But when John the Baptist and Christ Himself announced the need for repentance in light of the coming kingdom, it was these sinners who heeded the call. Christ says of them that "the children of this world are in their generation wiser than the children of light" (v. 8). Christ offers further explanation in verse 16 of the passage: "The law and the prophets were until John: since that time, the kingdom of God is preached, and every man presseth into it." The Pharisees, on the other hand, thinking of themselves as the children of light, showed a great lack of prudence as they rejected Christ's gospel calls and invitations.

The final point Christ makes concerns gospel reception. This point flows from another similarity between the steward of this parable and the prodigal son in the immediately preceding parable. The prodigal's plan worked in his favor (15:20–24); he was received back into his father's house (15:27). Likewise, the steward expects to be received into other houses (16:4). The implication is that he would be successful in finding favor with those to whom he ingratiated himself. So, too, those who return to the Lord in true repentance will surely be received.

The Savior

The Savior ultimately is the one who welcomes unjust stewards who flee to Him into the house of His gospel grace. Just as the master commended the steward for his prudence, so too Christ is commending and defending the publicans and sinners who were fleeing to Him (Luke 15:1–2). At the same time, Christ speaks this parable so that covetous and self-righteous Pharisees would realize that they have mismanaged their stewardship as profoundly as the publicans and sinners and to show how they need gospel prudence to abandon their self-righteousness and press into the kingdom.

Unlike the man of this parable, Christ Himself was a faithful steward. He perfectly managed all that His Father had given him to do (see John 17:4). Nevertheless, in His suffering and death, He suffered the judgment for all the mismanagement of all His people. He was put out of the Father's house, and there were none to receive him. On the basis of His active and passive obedience, believers now have a stewardship in community with all God's people, in which they use the resources entrusted to them to seek to bring others into the kingdom of heaven. They do so only from out of the Savior and the imputation of His righteousness to their account.

The Searchlight

This parable searches us with respect to whether we have the gospel prudence to see that we have wasted the goods God has entrusted to us through our unjust stewardship. In the parable of the prodigal son, which immediately precedes this parable, the older brother shows us how covetousness often coexists with self-righteousness and pride. After all, he looked down on his younger brother for the way he had abused his father's goods, but it's clear from what he says that he covets material enjoyment as well: "Lo, these many years do I serve thee, neither transgressed I at any time thy commandment; and yet thou never gavest me a kid, that I might make merry with my friends" (15:29). We often think the Pharisees thought too much of the law, but in reality, they didn't think *enough* of the law. That's why Christ faces all of us with the stringent demands of the law: "It is easier for heaven and earth to pass, than one tittle of the law to fail" (16:17). With all their focus on law, the Pharisees did not see their sin against the law. Their view of God was too low; their view of themselves was too high. Their view of sin was not serious enough; their view of the law was not radical enough. That's why Christ openly accused them of being covetous.

When God converted Paul, who had been a Pharisee, He did it by applying to his heart the force of the tenth commandment, "Thou shalt not covet" (see Rom. 7:7–25). Although he thought of himself as spiritually alive, he came to see just how dead he really was, bereft of all real righteousness. He, the Pharisee, could now only plead for mercy.

How we need a gospel prudence to seek the only way of escape—and if we do this, we too will hear the Master's commendation in the end. We too will be graciously welcomed into favor. Do we see that the misery of hell awaits us if we are not saved? We need to press into the kingdom before it is too late. Pressing into the kingdom means to repent and believe the promise of God in Jesus Christ, that He alone is a perfect satisfaction for sin and a complete righteousness. Just like this steward "pressed" himself into the houses of these debtors through his scheme, so, as Christ says elsewhere, we ought to strive to enter into the kingdom through repentance and faith (Luke 13:24).

Questions

1. People have often commented that the way we handle our money is a real indication of our heart. What was the steward's heart problem, and how does it relate to the Pharisees' heart problem (16:15)?

2. Read Luke 12:15 and Colossians 3:5. Describe how subtly covetousness works in our hearts and how dangerous it is.

3. Like the prodigal, who had some apprehension of the possibility of being received back, this steward had some apprehension that he might be welcomed and received by others. How does this carry over when it comes to repentance?

4. Apply the three lessons of this parable to the life of Paul. How did he learn them? Read Acts 9, Romans 7, and Philippians 3 if you need to.

5. The elder brother of the previous parable also had friends (Luke 15:29). Discuss the differences between gospel friendship and Pharisaic friendship. How important is it to show the friendship of Christ to lost and perishing sinners? How can this be done?

The Glory of Kingdom Testimony

THE PARABLE OF THE
RICH MAN AND LAZARUS
(Luke 16:19–31)

Abraham saith unto him, They have Moses
and the prophets; let them hear them. And
he said, Nay, father Abraham: but if one went
unto them from the dead, they will repent. And
he said unto him, If they hear not Moses and
the prophets, neither will they be persuaded,
though one rose from the dead.

—LUKE 16:29–31

15

Some people speculate that this account of the rich man and Lazarus is an actual historical account rather than a parable. However, since it begins similarly to the previous parable about the unjust steward (Luke 16:1–18) and continues many of its themes, most Bible scholars do count this as one of Christ's parables.

In fact, it is important to interpret this parable alongside the previous two parables (the prodigal son and the unjust steward). All three focus on the Pharisees, who are rejecting the gospel, of which Christ and all of the Scriptures testify.

The Scenery

This parable is about a rich man and a beggar. At the outset it is worth noting that Christ gives one of them a name, the beggar Lazarus (literally, "God helps him"). If anything, you might have expected the rich man to be named, because people typically know the names of the rich and famous. Beggars are usually nameless. As with all His parables, however, Christ tells this parable in light of eternity, and Lazarus had a name "written in heaven" (Luke 10:20)—and that's the name that ultimately counts! In this connection, how significant it is that the rich man is called only the "rich man" during his time on earth. After death, he is simply a "he." Obviously, none of his riches could remain his after his death.

The Pharisees, whom Christ is still addressing in this parable, would have highly esteemed someone as wealthy as this man. Luke has noted earlier in this chapter that the Pharisees were covetous (16:14). They believed that riches were invariably a sign of God's favor. The rich man certainly enjoyed many earthly comforts and apparently set his heart upon them. He was well-dressed and lived lavishly. Outside his door lived a beggar, Lazarus, who ate scraps from his table. Lazarus was covered with sores and was a picture of misery. All this would have caused the Pharisees to render the verdict that the rich man was likely righteous, the poor man likely unrighteous.

According to Christ, God judged very differently. The rich man went to hell, the place of torment. Lazarus, on the other hand, was brought to heaven with all its comforts, to the bosom of Abraham. The rich man would never be able to escape his misery. The gulf between heaven and hell is fixed, and his sentence was irreversible. However, according to the parable, he lifted up his eyes and saw Abraham and Lazarus in paradise. In great thirst, he begged Abraham to send Lazarus with a drop of water to cool his tongue. But Abraham reminded him of the good things that he enjoyed in his lifetime and also of the great gulf that separated him from them now.

The rich man then begged Abraham to send Lazarus to his father's house, to warn his brothers about the dangers of hell so that they might be spared coming there. But Abraham reminded the rich man that his brothers had Moses and the prophets, which were enough to teach them what they needed to know about the life to come. If they would not heed those words, they would not heed one who rose from the dead either.

The Substance

The first lesson that the parable clearly teaches is that earthly privileges will not keep a person from going to hell. Some have thought that the rich man's sin was that he was rich. But neither the parable nor any passage in Scripture teaches that. It's true that riches are a snare. It's also true that it is easier for a camel to go through the eye of a needle than for a rich man to enter the kingdom of heaven. But as riches cannot save a person, neither can they, by themselves, condemn anyone to hell.

This rich man had another privilege besides his wealth. Notice that Abraham addressed him as a son (Luke 16:25). Like his brothers, he had evidently been raised with the Word of God, Moses and the prophets (16:31). Like the Pharisees to whom Christ was speaking in this chapter, he was likely a faithful and respected member of the synagogue. All these things were privileges. But he failed to improve them and to seek God's blessing upon them, and thus they did him no good in the end. Ironically, this son of Abraham never made it to Abraham's bosom in heaven. He lacked the faith of his father Abraham, who believed God and had it accounted to him for righteousness. The Scriptures do warn us that outward religious privileges do not always translate to inward reality: "They are not all Israel, which are of Israel" (Rom. 9:6). And so even though in life this rich man could have secured help in any need, he was now totally helpless in hell.

But the opposite is true of Lazarus. In life, he lacked many of the rich man's outward privileges, but as the meaning of the name *Lazarus* ("God helps him") suggests, he had a helper in the Lord. God had blessed him spiritually, and so he had something far better than the rich man: "Happy is he that hath the God of Jacob for his help, whose hope is in the LORD" (Ps. 146:5).

The second lesson is that even prayer will not get a person out of hell. Undoubtedly, the rich man had prayed during his life. After all, he was a son of Abraham. However, his prayers would probably have been like those of the Pharisee from another parable, who prayed with himself and said, "God, I thank thee, that I am not as other men" (Luke 18:11). If only the rich man had learned to pray truly for help and mercy during his life! Now that he was in hell, he cried out to Abraham, even saying in verse 27, "I pray thee...." But what the rich man was doing was not true prayer at all. He prayed for mercy, but he prayed to Abraham instead of to God. He prayed for relief from his punishment, but not for pardon. He understood that he was now in torment, from which he desperately wanted relief, but he didn't confess the guilt that brought him into that torment. And the irrevocable truth is that the gulf was fixed. In hell, prayer cannot and will not change anything.

Not even this man's request to Abraham that Lazarus be sent to his brothers was answered the way he wanted. Some have wondered how it could be that someone in hell would desire the salvation of others, and so they have speculated on the motives of the rich man with respect to his brothers. Did the rich man dread having his brothers in hell with him because he did not want to hear their accusations against him? The parable does not explain his motives. However, this much is clear: heaven will never listen to hell's demands. In his life, this rich man could have simply snapped his fingers, and water, wine, and all sorts of earthly blessings would immediately be his. In hell, however, not the slightest or even the most pious-sounding request can or will be heard.

The third lesson concerns what can keep a person from hell. The last four verses of the parable use four words that shed light on what *is* able to keep a person from going down into hell:

1. *Testimony.* The rich man requested that Lazarus "testify" to his brothers (v. 28). The term *to testify* is often used in the New Testament. It means to witness earnestly to the truth as it is in Jesus Christ. Christ (John 3:32) and the apostles (Acts 18:5) testified. The Scriptures (John 5:39) and the Holy Spirit (John 15:26) also testify to the truth of the gospel. Whatever the rich man's motive may have been, Scripture makes clear that if we are to escape hell, we do desperately need the testimony of the Scriptures and the inward testimony of the Holy Spirit in our consciences and hearts.

2. *Hearing.* Abraham responded to the rich man: "They have Moses and the prophets; let them *hear* them" (v. 29). To be delivered from going to hell, we need to truly hear the Scriptures, that is, to heed the calls that they contain.

3. *Repentance.* The rich man answered Abraham: "Nay, father Abraham: but if one went unto them from the dead, they will repent" (v. 30). Sadly, this man had tragically

refused to repent. But he did know that *repentance* was what his brothers needed. Indeed, true repentance will save a man from going down into hell.

4. *Persuasion.* The final words of the parable come from the lips of Abraham. "If they hear not Moses and the prophets, neither will they be *persuaded*, though one rose from the dead" (v. 31, emphasis added). Remember that Abraham, while in life, did not enjoy the privilege of having Moses and the prophets. However, he was a man of faith in God. As Hebrews 11:13 explicitly states, he was "persuaded" of the promises and died in faith. In this parable, he pointed out to the rich man, and thus he points out to us as well, the value and sufficiency of Scripture for salvation. We need to be persuaded that what the Word of God says about us, God, and the way of salvation is real and true. If only this son of Abraham had possessed a living faith and persuasion! It would have kept him from hell.

The Savior

The parable of the prodigal son ended with the elder son outside of the house where there was joy and gladness. Now, Christ pictures the rich man outside for all eternity. Hereby the Savior mercifully warns the Pharisees and all of us who hear His word that, while it is still the day of grace, we should repent lest we end up eternally outside and apart from God, in hell. Christ here is unveiling the glory of the gospel testimony. Christ emphasizes how perfectly it is aligned with the Scriptures ("Moses and the prophets"). They are sufficient to attest to the truth of the gospel that He has been bringing. Even a miracle like raising someone from the dead will not make people who reject the Scriptures believe the gospel. Later on in His earthly ministry, Christ raised a man with the exact name as this Lazarus, and the Pharisees proved the truth of this by their response (John 11:56–57). In fact, when Christ rose from the dead, the Sanhedrin only opposed the truth more fiercely.

What a contrast Christ is to the rich man of this parable! His life is so entirely in line with this gospel testimony. In fact, because of His coming into the world and His work in redemption, there is a gospel testimony, both from His lips as well as from Moses and the prophets before His incarnation. Though He was infinitely richer than this rich man, yet He became poor (2 Cor. 8:9). Moreover, He entered into the punishments of hell for all His people and secured an everlasting inheritance for them. On that basis, the angels gather every one of His children—no matter how humble and poor they have been in this life—and they enter heaven with Abraham, Moses, the prophets, Lazarus, and all the faithful. Not only that, but they will forevermore rejoice in the presence of their Savior, who delivered them from so great a death.

The Searchlight

In this parable the glory of gospel testimony searches our hearts. We have "Moses and the prophets." In fact, we have even more than that—we have the whole Scripture. We know about the Lazarus whom Christ raised from the dead. We have the record of Christ's own victory over hell and death. Yet, by nature everyone prefers to live by their own instincts and desires rather than by the Word of God. Don't we find that the world around us lifts up the lifestyle of the rich man to us in the media and advertising? A life like his quickly becomes the envy of the natural heart as the pleasures of the world so easily take hold of us. Eternity seems so far off and far away, and many comfort themselves that they can have a life of pleasure now and can still have heaven later.

This parable searches our hearts to discern whether we seek to mortify the principle of covetousness with the help of the Holy Spirit. It also presses upon our lives the principles of eternity, the Scriptures, faith, and Christ. There is a great gulf fixed between heaven and hell. You either have Christ as your portion, or you are without Christ and hell awaits you. It is not sufficient to have the Scripture in your homes or to profess to be a son of Abraham. We need to walk in the footsteps of Abraham—and possess the faith of Abraham—by grace. Without it, our funeral may be "honorable," but the everlasting fire will be horrible.

Questions

1. Draw up a list of the "good things" and the "evil things" that we read about in Luke 16:25 for both the rich man and Lazarus. Discuss what this says about how we should look at this life. Compare this with the message of Psalm 73.

2. Why did Christ speak more about hell than anyone else in the Bible? What value is there in preaching and studying the doctrine of hell?

3. Some form of the word *torment* occurs four times in this passage. Why did Christ repeat this word over and over? Someone has said that the hell of

hell will be "son, remember" (v. 25); explain what that person might have meant.

4. The rich man thinks that if someone rose from the dead, people would believe him. Is that what happened when Christ rose from the dead? Explain your answer.

5. How does Luke 16:31 prove the principle of the sufficiency of Scripture? What practical implications does this principle have?

The Glory of Kingdom Access

THREE PARABLES ABOUT PRAYER
(Luke 11:5–13; 18:1–14)

And I say unto you, Ask, and it shall be given you; seek, and ye shall find; knock, and it shall be opened unto you. For every one that asketh receiveth; and he that seeketh findeth; and to him that knocketh it shall be opened. If a son shall ask bread of any of you that is a father, will he give him a stone? or if he ask a fish, will he for a fish give him a serpent? Or if he shall ask an egg, will he offer him a scorpion? If ye then, being evil, know how to give good gifts unto your children: how much more shall your heavenly Father give the Holy Spirit to them that ask him?

—LUKE 11:9–13

16

Prayer has often been called "the breath of the soul." When God works spiritual life in our hearts, this new life evidences itself in true prayer. For instance, Scripture records that Paul began to pray after Christ appeared to him on the road to Damascus. Prior to this, he had undoubtedly *said* many prayers. After all, most people say a prayer at one time or another. However, the Lord notes Paul's new posture, one of *true* prayer, with the words, "Behold, he prayeth" (Acts 9:11). As the Heidelberg Catechism makes clear, true prayer is that which proceeds "from the heart" (A. 117).

For the Christian, however, prayer isn't just some thoughts cast heavenward. The Scriptures teach that by faith, the Christian, through prayer, has access to the throne of grace (Rom. 5:2; Eph. 2:18; 3:12; Heb. 4:15–16; 10:19). Yet it would be wrong to suggest that prayer is always easy for believers. In fact, the opposite is often the case. There are many hindrances to overcome when Christians go to prayer and persevere in it. God's Word honestly addresses these hindrances. In fact, Christ devoted at least three parables to the subject of prayer. In each one, He shows the glory of gospel access. Each time, His teaching addresses common hindrances to prayer. Clearly, when heeded, His teaching fosters gospel access. Let's take each of the parables in turn, this time treating the scenery and substance together for each one.

The Friend at Midnight (Luke 11:5–13)

Christ had just given the Lord's Prayer to His disciples, who had asked Him, "Lord, teach us to pray" (Luke 11:1). Christ then tells the parable of a man who received an unexpected guest in the middle of the night. The man went to a nearby friend to ask for some bread to serve his guest. Even though his friend was in bed, the man overcame any hesitancy he might have felt, went to the friend's house, and woke him up. The pressing need of the moment, combined with his confidence in his friendship with his neighbor, caused the man to set usual decorum aside, even though the hour was so late.

It is easy to imagine both this man's sense of need and his neighbor's willingness to help. But Christ mentions two specific reasons for the neighbor's generosity. First, the man at the door was his friend, and friends are obliged to help each other in times of need. Everyone understands that. But, second, even if friendship would not have motivated this neighbor to help, the sense of urgency that was evident in the man's coming at midnight with his request would have been enough. Christ says it this way: "Yet because of his importunity he will rise and give him as many as he needeth" (11:8).

Christ is addressing a common hindrance in prayer, the feeling that the Lord is indifferent to us and our prayers. We doubt that the Lord is truly concerned about us. This can be such a crippling thing for believers. Despite all the promises in the Bible, and despite how often the Lord has heard and answered our prayers, we still imagine that God is not concerned about us. This feeling can overwhelm believers to the point that they do not pray—or do not pray in faith.

So if you would quite easily disturb your friend in an emergency and expect that he would help you, is there then not even more reason to go to the Lord, who neither sleeps nor slumbers (Ps. 121:4)? He cares more for believers than any friend could. Should we then be reluctant to pray? It's no wonder that the Lord follows this parable with these words: "Ask, and it shall be given you; seek, and ye shall find; knock, and it shall be opened unto you" (Luke 11:9). There can be no doubt: this parable aims to foster gospel access by reassuring believers of the fatherly care of the Lord. "If a son shall ask bread of any of you that is a father, will he give him a stone? Or if he ask a fish, will he for a fish give him a serpent?" (11:11). So Christ shows the glory of gospel access for timid believers.

The Persistent Widow (Luke 18:1–8)

A second hindrance to prayer is the feeling that our prayers, up to this point, have gone unanswered. It is connected to the first hindrance, in a sense; we ultimately end up thinking that the Lord is indifferent to us because He is not answering our prayers. In essence, both hindrances are forms of unbelief. The perception that God will not hear us or is not hearing us stifles prayer.

Christ gives the parable about the persistent widow, which addresses this second hindrance. Luke explicitly specifies the purpose of the parable as follows: "that men ought always to pray, and not to faint" (v. 1). The parable tells about a widow who had suffered some injustice or wrongdoing.

Her only recourse was a corrupt judge, someone who feared neither God nor man. The widow continued to trouble the judge until he helped her. He helped her not because he cared about her, but only because he didn't want to be bothered by her anymore. The parable concludes: "And shall not God avenge his own elect, which cry day and night unto him, though he bear long with them?" (v. 7).

The point of the parable is clear. Though the judge was unjust, the widow received her request because of her persistence. And would the believer, who comes not only to a perfectly just judge (see Gen. 18:25) but also a gracious heavenly Father, find persistent prayer to be fruitless? The answer is clear: of course not. Gospel access is sure by virtue of God's character. It's true—the Lord can delay for His own wise reasons. But isn't it often our own delays and doubts that keep us from praying? By revealing the Lord as so infinitely better than an unjust judge, Christ gives this parable to foster gospel access for the discouraged believer.

The Pharisee and the Publican (Luke 18:9–15)

One of the most subtle hindrances to prayer is a sense of self-sufficiency. We may think that we're doing fine with regard to our souls and our lives in general. As a result, we do not feel the need for earnest prayer. This attitude of self-sufficiency is different from the previous two hindrances to prayer that we have discussed. But it has the same effect: it quenches true prayer.

Christ addresses this hindrance in His well-known parable of the Pharisee and the publican. Notice that He says that *two* men went up to the temple to pray. However, when it really came down to it, the Pharisee had only a form of prayer and in the end doesn't actually pray *for* anything. He simply expressed his own self-sufficiency under the guise of speaking to God.

Christ addresses this devastating hindrance to prayer by showing the heart of true prayer. Both the publican's posture before God and the words he spoke evidence this. He smote upon his breast. He confessed that he was but a sinner, and in his brokenness he cried out to God for mercy. And this simple but heartfelt prayer brought down God's approval upon him, along with an infinite number of blessings. In fact, you could say that this publican in prayer laid hold on all the riches of God's covenant—for that is what mercy is—with his simple and sincere prayer. And so Christ again fosters gospel access by revealing God as a merciful God, easily entreated by those who cast themselves on His promise for mercy.

The Savior

In this parable Christ unveils Himself in terms of gospel access to His Father. He still does this today in His people's lives. From heaven, He sees them struggling with hindrances to prayer, and He removes them by His Word and Spirit so as to give gospel access to His Father. He is pleased with His people's persistent, humble, eager prayers. He is also their heavenly intercessor, praying for them before the throne of grace. Heaven has so many mercies of which earth is so needy.

See all the ways in which Christ unveils Himself. In the first parable, Christ is the "Reason" the Father can answer His people's importunate prayers. For the sake of Christ, the Elder Brother, God can and will hear His people as their

able and willing Father (Luke 11:11–13). Second, because
of Christ's work on the cross, His Father is quite the opposite of the unjust judge. In fact, He will speedily avenge His
people (Luke 18:7–8). After all, Christ is His people's advo-
cate (1 John 2:1), and for His work's sake, the Father Himself
loves them (John 16:27). Third, it is for Christ's sake that
the verdict of "justified" (Luke 18:14) can be pronounced
upon praying beggars like the publican. God's mercy comes
to them by way of Calvary, where Christ, "who knew no sin,"
became sin, in order that those who beg with mercy can
"be made the righteousness of God in him" (2 Cor. 5:21).
Through *Him* there is gospel access.

The Searchlight

How these glorious parables expose our hearts! The problem with our prayerlessness is our wrong or small thoughts
of God. Our hearts often think He is less than a friendly
neighbor. He is worse than an unjust judge. He is less than a
God who delights in mercy. How simple prayer really should
be to us! After all, what simple pictures Christ used in these
parables—a needy man at midnight, a needy widow, and a
needy sinner in the temple. Notice the common thread: they
were *needy*. If only we sensed our desperate need more, we
would pray more readily, more persistently, more humbly.
And don't you think we would receive more readily all that
God wishes to give?

On the other hand, the portrait of the Pharisee shows us
the danger of a spirit of self-sufficiency, even among believers. What a hindrance this is to gospel access! How we need
to be kept needy! How we need Christ's Spirit to be poured

upon us again and again, in order that we might pray as we ought (Rom. 8:26).

Questions

1. Hindrances in prayer often come with a faulty view of God. Each parable we have looked at helps correct a wrong understanding of who God is. Discuss what these wrong understandings are.

2. In Luke 11:9, the word *importunity* literally means "shamelessness." Can prayers that are "shamelessly" bold still be reverent?

3. Why does Christ conclude the parable of the persistent widow with the question, "Nevertheless when the Son of man cometh, shall he find faith on the earth?" (Luke 18:8). What does this have to do with prayer?

4. Compare and contrast the Pharisee and the publican—the spirit, content, and result of each of their prayers. Does the fact that the parable describes both men make it more powerful?

5. What other hindrances to prayer can you think of, and can you think of other parables or passages that address those hindrances?

The Glory of Kingdom Consummation:
More Parables from Matthew

The Glory of Kingdom Forgiveness

THE PARABLE OF THE
UNFORGIVING SERVANT
(Matthew 18:23–35)

Then his lord, after that he had called him, said
unto him, O thou wicked servant, I forgave thee
all that debt, because thou desiredst me: shoul-
dest not thou also have had compassion on thy
fellowservant, even as I had pity on thee?
—MATTHEW 18:32–33

~ 17 ~

Most people are not completely unforgiving of others. After all, who doesn't overlook small faults and grievances? But all of us can relate to Peter's question in this passage: "Lord, how oft shall my brother sin against me, and I forgive him? till seven times?" (Matt. 18:21).

The context of this parable is Christ's teaching His disciples about church life and church discipline. Christ's will is that His church be a place of humility and service. It should also be a place in which there is joy when straying disciples return (see Matt. 18:13). And if one brother sins against another brother, there should be reconciliation through truth and repentance (see Matt. 18:22).

At this point, Peter raises his practical question: "How often should I forgive someone before I can say, 'Enough is enough—I can't forgive you any longer?'" It is reported that the rabbis specified that forgiveness should be offered as many as three times. (It is interesting that today we have the saying, "Three strikes and you're out.") So Peter's suggestion of *seven times* seems generous. But Christ answers Peter: Not seven times, but "seventy times seven" (v. 22). In order to explain what He means and press it home, Christ speaks the parable before us. Our forgiveness of a repenting brother or sister must be unlimited, much like the kingdom forgiveness that God applies to believers is unlimited, or unbounded. In fact, *our* forgiveness should stem from God's forgiveness.

The Scenery

This parable is often separated into three scenes. The first scene (vv. 23–27) introduces us to two of its main characters. On the one hand, there was a wealthy king. This king wanted to settle accounts with his servants. It isn't clear whether his servants were tax collectors, money handlers, or officials in his kingdom. But we can assume that at least one particular servant, the second main character, dealt with a lot of the king's financial resources, since he somehow accumulated a great debt that he owed the king. Christ says the servant owed the king ten thousand talents, which was an exorbitant amount of money. Commentators say that this man owed anywhere from 150 thousand to 200 thousand years' worth of wages to the king, something equivalent to several billion dollars today. He clearly didn't have the money to repay this great debt, so the king ordered the servant and his family to be sold into slavery. In desperation, the man fell down before the king (v. 26) and begged him to have patience with him. He promised to pay everything he owed. In response, the king forgave him his large debt!

The second scene (vv. 28–31) introduces the third main character, a second servant. The first servant, who had just been forgiven his exorbitant debt, found this second servant, who owed him money, and demanded payment. Although this second servant's debt was substantially smaller than his own, the first servant quickly resorted to physical violence, grabbing his debtor by the throat. The second servant pleaded with the first servant to have patience with him. He used exactly the same words the first servant used when he begged for mercy from the king. But, apparently, the first servant did not hear the echo of his own predicament. He ordered the second servant to be taken away and put in prison until he could pay his debt. It seems that the king's other servants, knowing what had happened with the first servant's debt, were so bothered by this turn of events that they brought word back to the king.

The third scene is the climax of the parable (vv. 32–35). The king summoned the first servant. In light of how this servant has treated his debtor, the king ordered him to be taken away and tortured until he had paid his entire debt. Christ then concludes by showing that the king represents His Father, and the parable is meant to warn the disciples of the consequences of not forgiving "from your hearts...every one his brother their trespasses" (v. 35).

The Substance

As we consider the substance of this parable, it is important to notice that Christ is not teaching the way of salvation. He is not teaching that we are forgiven of our sins only because we forgive others or that once someone has been forgiven by God, it is possible for that person to lose his forgiveness. These ideas contradict what Scripture teaches elsewhere about the forgiveness of sins and the way of salvation.

Instead, Christ is teaching about something that should be a result of salvation. Remember, in this chapter He is focusing on matters of church life and church discipline. He teaches about confronting, disciplining, and receiving offending brothers and sisters back into the fellowship of the church. This parable is a clear demonstration of the truths Christ is teaching. The huge debt the first servant owed the king symbolizes a debt of sin.

Notice that Christ states that the king "forgave" the servant that debt. We could say that this corresponds with the general declaration of forgiveness set forth in the gospel. But the proclamation of the availability of pardon should not be confused with the actual pardoning of sin. In the sinner's heart must be true faith, which embraces such a benefit with a believing heart. If we are truly justified in this way, we also receive a new nature, which becomes evident through sanctification. Divine grace works in the heart and produces fruits in the life of the justified sinner. One of these fruits should be an attitude of unbounded kingdom forgiveness to those who sin against us. Think of David, who, after receiving mercy from God, looked for someone to whom he could show the "mercy of God" (2 Sam. 9:3).

On the other hand, if we continue to hold a brother's sin against him and find no room in our hearts for mercy and forgiveness, we are acting like the hypocritical first servant in the parable. We are standing over our brother in judgment. This evidences that our own heart is not right with God.

The Savior

Christ unveils Himself in this parable as it pertains to kingdom forgiveness. See Him first as a meticulous Savior. The massive debt the first servant owed the king is explicitly and accurately stated as ten thousand talents; we are not just given an approximate amount. As I stated previously, this man's debt represents a debt of sin. We can learn from this that our sins are explicitly and accurately tallied. Although we may fail to recognize or count our own sins, they are all written in God's book. And when Christ went to Calvary to pay for the sins of His people, He took every one of those sins upon Himself there. His sacrifice for sin was not an imprecise or approximate payment for those sins. Rather, His death covered *every* sin His people have ever committed. He knew what sins—and how many—He was dying for when He laid down His life for His sheep.

See Him secondly as a gracious Savior. I've already mentioned that Jesus is not teaching the way of salvation in this parable. Rather, He is highlighting the result of the true experience of salvation. Yet it is noteworthy that Christ teaches this parable as He is on His way to the cross. Forgiveness of sin is only possible on the basis of His mediatorial sacrifice at Calvary. He is the only Savior of sinners. It is good news that is proclaimed in the gospel, namely, that "there is forgiveness with thee, that thou mayest be feared" (Ps. 130:4). Not everyone who thinks he is forgiven is actually forgiven, but that is not because of a shortage of forgiveness with God. We find it very difficult to forgive the same person three times, much less seven times, but in His mercy, God through Christ casts all the sins of His people "into the depths of the sea" (Mic. 7:19).

See Him thirdly as a judging Savior. Those who abuse His gospel in order to continue in sin and hardness of heart will meet the wrath of the slighted Lamb. This is clearly seen in the king's final treatment of the first servant. His declaration of mercy is removed from the servant, who is then handed over to be tormented until his unpayable debt is paid.

Psalm 2:12 says, "Kiss the Son, lest he be angry, and ye perish from the way, when his wrath is kindled but a little."

The Searchlight

The glory of this parable searches and exposes our hearts in three respects:

1. *Our insurmountable debt of sin.* The law demands strict obedience. Its every jot and tittle must be fulfilled. By nature, we break God's law constantly, consistently, and easily. To use the language of this parable, our debt quickly runs into the billions and exceeds anything we could ever pay back. We need the work of the Holy Spirit to see our sin as God sees it and to feel the sting of our helpless and dire predicament. Truly, our only hope is to have the kingdom forgiveness God applies in the gospel for Christ's sake.

2. *Our double standard with respect to others and ourselves.* How often have we metaphorically stood with our hands around an offending brother's or sister's "neck" while ignoring our own sin before God, which is infinitely worse? In order to loosen our grip on the "throats" of others and grant this kingdom forgiveness easily and quickly, we should think often of our great debt before God.

3. *Our need of Christ.* In order to show this kingdom forgiveness to others, we need the forgiving grace of God in Christ for ourselves. But we also need His enabling grace to forgive in an unbounded way.

Questions

1. What is the difference between "seven times" and seventy times seven, both mathematically and spiritually?

2. The king's other servants were bothered (Matt. 18:31). Does this have any connection with the church discipline spoken of in verse 17?

3. Must we forgive a brother or sister who is not repentant?

4. Can the Lord revoke His forgiveness? How then do you explain verse 34?

5. Isn't it a contradiction to say that Christ is both a merciful Savior and a judging, emphasis added Savior? Explain your answer.

6. What would you say to a person who claims that unbounded kingdom forgiveness is not realistically possible?

The Glory of Kingdom Grace

THE PARABLE OF THE
LABORERS IN THE VINEYARD
(Matthew 20:1–16)

So the last shall be first, and the first last: for
many be called, but few chosen.

—MATTHEW 20:16

~ *18* ~

Once I heard a preacher say something like this: "Many believe in salvation by grace, but to them grace is not grace. When I ask them to spell grace, they spell it this way: 'w-o-r-k-s.'" This statement gets at the lesson of this parable. Is our view of God, Christ, and salvation such that we adore God's free grace? Or do we carry over a works attitude, even as we talk about grace? In other words, is grace truly grace to us?

The Scenery

In many ways, the picture Christ paints in this parable would have been a very realistic one to His audience. Their work-day was considered to be from sunrise to sunset, about twelve hours. It was common for those who did not have steady employment to gather in the marketplace, where employers would come and hire workers for the day. In our day, we would call this a job fair, though back then it was far more primitive. At the end of the day, the employer would pay out the wage in accordance with the biblical requirement (Lev. 19:13; Deut. 24:14–15). The coin Christ refers to was the denarius (the Greek is translated "penny" in this passage). The denarius was indeed a typical wage for a day's work. It wasn't a generous wage, but it would help a worker meet some of his basic needs.

Though the picture would have been a familiar one for the original audience, one element of the story would have been very surprising. Each laborer received an equal wage, regardless of whether he had worked all twelve hours of the day, or only one hour. The householder's generosity toward those who worked only part of the day would have been unusual. But this is intentional on Christ's part and will be a point of instruction for His hearers.

The Substance

The parable's context helps us understand its basic message. Just before giving the parable, the Lord Jesus had three interactions. Each of those interactions demonstrates a basic misunderstanding of the gospel. First, Jesus' disciples tried to turn away little children, who had been brought by their mothers for a blessing from Him (Matt. 19:13–15). Second, there was a rich young man who wanted to know what he could do to inherit eternal life. He went away sorrowful after Jesus told him to sell all his possessions and give the money to the poor. He was unwilling to part with his riches (19:16–22). Then, Christ's disciples came on the scene again. This time, they were looking for rewards for the sacrifices they had made in following Christ (19:23–30). These people did not understand that the blessings of Christ are given freely, out of gospel grace; they are not deserved and cannot be earned.

Christ hints that this is the basic point of the parable by what He says immediately preceding it: "Many that are first shall be last; and the last shall be first" (19:30). In other words, there are people who think they deserve to be treated as first; yet, precisely because they think they have something coming to them, they will end up last. Christ speaks similar words at the end of the parable (20:16): "So the last shall be first, and the first last: for many be called, but few chosen." And so we can conclude that, as He tells this parable, Christ is targeting those who believe that they deserve or can somehow earn salvation, favor, or blessing.

At the end of the day, when the householder handed out wages, the workers who had worked all day "murmured against the goodman of the house" (20:11). They felt that the householder was unjust to pay those who had worked only part of the day the same wage as they earned. But they had no right to feel unjustly treated. The householder had been fair, fulfilling his agreement with them. They were clearly bitter about the generosity he showed to those who had worked fewer hours. The way they perceived the householder's actions suggested that their hearts were not in the right place. The householder asked one of them, "Is thine eye evil, because I am good?" (v. 15). In other words, "Don't you see that the way you are looking at this is twisted and wrong? You are misreading my generosity to others as unfairness to you." That's what the householder meant.

The perception the first group of laborers had essentially grew from the soil of pride. Pride loves to earn a standing with God. It thinks it can dictate what God should or should not do. The householder pinpointed this pride when he asked, "Is it not lawful for me to do what I will with mine own?" (v. 15). Essentially, these first laborers were sitting in judgment over the householder. They basically gave themselves the right to dictate what he did with his own money. None of these workers might have put it like that, but that was in effect what they were doing. This was unbounded pride.

The parable is teaching us two postures that do fit with how God's kingdom of grace operates:

1. *Thankful joy*—If the laborers who had started at 6:00 a.m. had been as generous and kind-spirited as their householder, they would have rejoiced that other laborers were brought in to help. They should have been happy that others had been invited into the vineyard instead of being left to stand idly and carelessly in the market square. They should have been glad that these day laborers had come into relationship with this benevolent householder. They should have been happy that these others did not need to go to sleep hungry, but instead had their basic needs met.

2. *Gospel trust*—Notice how the second, third, and fourth groups simply worked out of an attitude of trust in the householder's promise. He said, "Whatsoever is right, that shall ye receive" (v. 7). They trusted his character and his word, without needing the promise of a specific wage. Especially the fourth and final group could hardly have expected much of a wage at all. By 5:00 p.m., they might have given up any hope of making any wage that day. Their thankfulness to the householder would have been greater than that of those who were hired at the beginning of the day, who trusted that their toil through the long hours of the wearying day would bring them a reward.

The Savior

Christ unveils His glory in this parable as it pertains to kingdom grace. See, first, in what gracious light Christ puts the householder. Thus Christ shows His disciples a far more excellent mindset than they were displaying. How troubling it must have been to Christ to hear His disciples put themselves above others, like Peter did just prior to this passage: "Behold, we have forsaken all, and followed thee; what shall we have therefore?" (Matt. 19:27). His question showed an attitude that was totally foreign to the Lord, whose thoughts were perfectly aligned with His Father's. After telling this parable, Christ spoke of how He would soon go to the cross (Matt. 20:20–28). There He would purchase a kingdom and secure redemption for every one of His people, Peter included. Because of that purchase, redemption would be full and free. It is especially on the cross that God in Christ shows how good and gracious a householder He is. The householder can say, "I am good" (v. 15), because Christ gave His life that He might freely bestow upon His people a gracious bounty.

Second, see how Christ enables His people to root out legalism and display a gracious spirit to others. We need Christ to teach us that laboring in His vineyard is not a drudgery that deserves proportionate compensation. If we have that kind of an attitude, we are not living out of free grace. When Christ indwells our hearts, we begin to see how infinitely gracious the Lord is even to pluck us out of the "idleness" of sin and put us to labor in His vineyard. It is more than enough to be in fellowship with Him. May Christ rid us of this evil notion that we deserve more than we have, and may He fill our hearts with the overwhelming goodness of the Lord.

The Searchlight

The parable radically exposes the self-righteous bent our minds have by nature, even after they have received grace. It is not difficult to relate to the perception of the workers who had worked the full day. We can easily have the same sense of injustice when we see others getting off "easier" than we do.

How often we feel like we have toiled in the sweat of our faces, bearing the burden and heat of the day. "Others around us haven't had to work so hard," we tell ourselves, "and see how God blesses them!" We must guard against a proud spirit. How pride blinds us to itself! The professing church has many who think that what they have done for God and the kingdom entitles them to greater benefits, honors, and accolades. In essence, they are lording it over God and seeking to take Him off His throne.

Many imagine that Christ should be happy with them and their efforts. Theologically speaking, we could say that they are still operating under the framework of the covenant of works, thinking that even in religion, they *act* in order to *attain*; they *do* in order to *deserve*; they *go* in order to *get*.

What Christ is teaching us here is that we ought rather to be enflamed by the reality of gospel grace. If only the disciples, instead of thinking themselves deserving and the children undeserving, had welcomed them to be blessed by Christ. If only the rich young man had sold all that he had in order to follow Christ, who had left all the treasures of heaven to come to earth. If only the man had by faith exchanged his futile self-righteousness for a relationship with Christ, through whom he would have known and experienced gospel grace. If only the disciples, instead of worrying about what reward they might receive for all their sacrifices here, had basked in the presence of their Lord and Master now, and left the present and the future to Him. If only the laborers who were called first would have been as thankful and trusting as the eleventh-hour laborers and as good-hearted as the householder himself.

If we are converted either early in life or at the eleventh hour, let us be thankful for kingdom grace and trust God's faithful gospel promise. If we have left all and followed Him, let us always trust and rejoice in the fact that—thanks be to God—He does what pleases Him. If we believe these things, we will be debtors to God's marvelous grace forever.

Questions

1. Many try to spiritualize the different hours and groups and items mentioned in this parable. They say that the first group was the Jews, or that the denarius is eternal life, etc. Show how you will have problems if you start spiritualizing all the details (for example, do we really work for a reward? were these first laborers truly saved?). Review the major point of the parable.

2. How do you harmonize the message of the parable of the ten virgins, where the wise virgins had extra oil, with this parable, in which it seems that idleness and carelessness for so long does not matter?

3. In what subtle ways do we show the attitude of the laborers who were first hired in our relationships, in the church, in other areas of our lives?

4. What do you make of the householder's going back time and again to take idle people into his service? What does this tell us about Christ?

5. Reflect on Christ's question: "Is thine eye evil, because I am good?" (20:15). Think of biblical or contemporary examples of how God's revelation of grace does frequently bring out the evil judgments of man.

The Glory of Kingdom Design

THE PARABLE OF THE WICKED HUSBANDMEN
(Matthew 21:33–46)

Last of all he sent unto them his son, saying,
They will reverence my son. But when the
husbandmen saw the son, they said among
themselves, This is the heir; come, let us kill
him, and let us seize on his inheritance. And
they caught him, and cast him out of the vineyard, and slew him. When the lord therefore
of the vineyard cometh, what will he do unto
those husbandmen?

—MATTHEW 21:37–40

19

I once was in a house that was built right next to a quarry. On the main floor was an unusual step up into a side room. The owner of the house explained that when the house had been built, there was a rock outcropping there. It would have been very difficult to get rid of it, so the builders decided to make this one room with a step up in order to get around it. In this parable, Christ exhibits Himself as the rock that no one can ultimately get around. All of us must reckon with Christ, and we will, one way or another. God has made Him to be the stone on which we must build or over whom we will stumble. That is how He has designed the kingdom. The ultimate question still remains: "What think ye of Christ?" (Matt. 22:42).

The Scenery
Christ tells this parable in the last week before His crucifixion. Matthew, Mark (12:1–12), and Luke (20:9–19) all record this parable, and the slight variations in details can easily be harmonized. Among all the parables, this one refers most clearly and explicitly to the death of Christ.

The basic picture of the parable is a vineyard, a comparison that the Bible regularly uses for the people of God (see Isa. 5:1–7; Song 8:11–12). However, the focus in this parable is on those entrusted with leadership among the people of

God, who are referred to as the husbandmen. This is confirmed in verse 45: "And when the chief priests and Pharisees had heard his parables, they perceived that he spake of them."

This parable does more, however, than just speak about what the chief priests and Pharisees of that day were doing. In fact, this parable gives us a picture of how to understand all of human history. It tells of how God has sent His servants, time and time again, to receive the fruits man owes to Him. Think of the prophets God sent, whom Israel mistreated. In the end, God sent His Son, who was killed by wicked men. Do you see how the parable summarizes all of human history up to the cross of Christ? And after He tells the parable, Christ goes on to speak of what God would do after the cross, in raising His Son from the dead. Seen this way, the parable is universal in that it covers all of history and has a message for all people.

The Substance

The key to understanding this parable can be found in the relationship of *Son* and *stone*. In Hebrew there is only one letter difference between the words for "son" (*ben*) and "stone" (*eben*). In this parable, Christ reveals Himself as both. On the one hand, He is the Son of God, sent by God that we might reverence Him (v. 37). On the other hand, He is also the stone of the corner, on which the whole structure of God's building rests. Just as it is dangerous for a laborer not to respect the son of the owner and for a carpenter to ignore an unmovable stone, so too not to reverence the Son of God will be our ruin.

Our sinful natures try to get around Christ, but we end up stumbling all our lives long unless we recognize that He is the stone, set up by God to be the cornerstone on which we must build. He must be *reverenced*—or we will never prosper. This is what this parable teaches.

Despite what common courtesy dictates, the husbandmen (or tenants) in the parable did not respect the owner, his servants, or his son. These tenants terribly abused the king's servants first. Then the king sent his own son to them, assuming that they would reverence him. But verse 37 exposes their evil intentions. There we hear the husbandmen say, "This is the heir, come, let us kill him, and let us seize on his inheritance" (v. 38). What arrogance and insanity! It's no wonder that when Christ asks what the owner will do when he comes (v. 40), the answer is obvious: "He will miserably destroy those wicked men, and will let out his vineyard unto other husbandmen" (v. 41).

From a certain perspective, the parable could have ended with verse 41. In that case, the ending scene would have been the son's dead body hanging outside the vineyard, with the king's army on its way to judge the wicked husbandmen. However, the parable doesn't end there, for, if it had, there would be no gospel in the parable. But Christ was keen to speak, not just of His coming death but of God's kingdom design in and through His death.

In order to do that, Christ quotes the Old Testament, as He often did, proving that the gospel was not a new thing but was designed and prophesied before it was accomplished. He quotes from Psalm 118, which, as part of the Passover liturgy, would have been on the minds of the Passover pilgrims at this time of the year. "The stone which the builders rejected, the same is become the head of the corner: this is the Lord's doing, and it is marvellous in our eyes" (v. 42; compare Ps. 118:22–23).

The Savior

Christ unveils Himself in this parable in a remarkable way. First, we should view Him as a seer (or prophet). Christ here is predicting His own death and revealing its significance. As I mentioned, no other parable refers so clearly and explicitly to the death of Christ. Christ is telling beforehand what will soon happen to Him. He is also showing how His death fits into all of history.

Second, we should see him as son. His death is the death of the son at the hands of wicked men, specifically, of the leaders to whom the Lord had entrusted the vineyard of His visible church. Though God has every reason to expect that men would honor His Son, this is not the case. However, this is not outside the Father's plan or scope. The cross of Christ comes forth from the Father and is endured by the Son, not merely as a tragedy, but as part of the divine plan of redemption. Think of what Peter says in Acts 2: "Him, being delivered by the determinate counsel and foreknowledge of God, ye have taken, and by wicked hands have crucified and slain: Whom God hath raised up…" (vv. 23–24).

Third, we should see him as the stone. Christ intentionally moves from the picture of Himself as "son" to the "stone" of the corner. He is not just predicting His own death; He is also picturing His vindication in His resurrection. Psalm 118 is a messianic psalm in which the psalmist, who trusts in the Lord, is beleaguered by many enemies (vv. 5–13a). Yet the Lord does not put him to shame, but vindicates him (v. 13b–21) and even makes the stone that the builders foolishly reject the corner-stone of the whole building of God. By referencing these verses on the heels of His parable, Christ changes the scene from a *vineyard* to a *building*. The wicked religious leaders of God's vineyard will not succeed. God is above and beyond them, and His purposes will prevail. Though they cast the Son out of the vineyard, it is He who will be the approved stone for a new building of God. Thus God will receive the honor He deserves, and Christ will as well—now not just as son, but as the vindicated, honorable stone.

The Searchlight

This parable is highly searching, not just of its original audience, but of us as well, and it obliges us to consider three questions:

1. *Do we honor God and Christ, whom He has sent?* As our creator, God has a right to receive fruit from us. Especially in the visible church, God has hedged us about with His precepts, ordinances, and institutions. These things testify of His care for us and of His will that we should render Him our lives, as fruit to His honor. By nature, however, we do not yield Him any fruit, nor do we give Him the honor He deserves. Especially those who have been appointed to be leaders in the visible church bring guilt upon themselves when they neglect, despise, and reject God and His Son, and instead crave honor for themselves. Do we take seriously the call to reverence the Son of God? It is the height of sin not to do so.

2. *Do we humbly adore God's kingdom design?* When the Lord says, "They will reverence my Son," this is not simply

the wish of an otherwise powerless God. God's design does not terminate with man's rejection of Him or His Son. Even through the rejection of His Son, His cause is furthered. That cause cannot fail. The Father has ensured that by raising His Son from the dead. The very stone, rejected by men as unfit to be used in building, the Lord made to be the stone of the corner. Everything will be built on Him, or it will not be built at all. Thus God brings double honor to Himself, for His designs do not depend on man, but are furthered despite him, and against all odds. This should make us wonder at the might and grace of the Lord. It should also make us repent of our sin and unbelief, through which we have rejected the Son whom He has sent.

3. *Are our lives built on Christ, the cornerstone?* The Hebrew word *honor* literally means "to be heavy." If our lives do not reverence the Son, we have every reason to expect God's heavy judgment. If we are not built on Christ, the cornerstone, we will be destroyed (v. 44). There is no getting around Him. Imagine a builder who foolishly tries to ignore the cornerstone and build next to it. He is going to be constantly tripping over the cornerstone, but he will not get it to move.

Questions

1. Read Isaiah 5:1–7. There is a similarity and a difference between this parable and the parable told there. Discuss the relationship between the two.

2. What does reverencing the Son involve? In order to answer this, compare this parable with Psalm 2:6–12.

3. The apostle Peter must have heard Christ tell this parable. Discuss in what ways 1 Peter 2:1–8 further explains what it means to honor the Son.

4. Think about what it meant to Christ to be just days away from His death on the cross. Discuss this both from the perspective of the shame He was to face as well as the honor that would be given Him.

5. Why do we by nature stumble over Christ rather than honor Him? What practical difference does it make in our lives that Christ's honor is sure?

The Glory of Kingdom Watchfulness

THE PARABLE OF THE TEN VIRGINS
(Matthew 25:1–13)

At midnight there was a cry made, Behold, the
bridegroom cometh; go ye out to meet him.
—MATTHEW 25:6

20

Who does not look forward with excitement to a wedding? Although it may have happened, I have never heard of anyone oversleeping and missing a wedding they were to attend. It would be especially unfortunate if a bridegroom or bride missed his or her own wedding! We would definitely call such a person a fool. Yet there are people who will be found to be foolish when it comes to the great wedding at the end of time. Christ pictures for us five such fools. They were not only asleep, but also terribly unprepared for the greatest wedding of all.

The Scenery

Those who heard Christ preach this parable could easily have imagined its setting. The ten virgins in this parable would have gathered as attendants of the bride at her home shortly before the wedding ceremony, waiting for the procession to the groom's house, where the ceremony would take place. They were holding torches, long poles with oil lamps tied to the top. The bridegroom, however, did not arrive at the bride's house to pick her up as soon as anticipated. When he finally arrived, only five of the ten virgins were able to accompany him to his home and enter the marriage supper. The central message of the parable is bound up with the separa-

tion that occurs with this group of attendants because some
are ready and some are not.

The Substance

This parable depicts the visible church as ten virgins. *All
ten* of them were invited to participate in the wedding. *All
ten* of them would have responded positively to the wedding
invitation. *All ten* of them attended the bride on the way
to the wedding feast. *All ten* of them had lamps, which at
first gave light. Finally, *all ten* grew drowsy and fell asleep
when the bridegroom's coming was delayed. So how did the
group get separated?

Christ describes the events that separated five of these
virgins from their companions. First, as the coming of the
bridegroom was delayed (v. 5), some of them ran out of oil.
Second, it was specifically the cry announcing the imminent
arrival of the bridegroom (v. 6) that sent five virgins scram-
bling for oil, thus taking them away. Third, shutting the
door to the wedding (v. 10) made a final separation between
the two groups.

What, however, was the root cause of the separation?
Early in the parable, we are told that five of the virgins were
wise, while the other five were foolish (v. 2). Those who were
wise "took [extra] oil in their vessels with their lamps," while
those who were foolish "took their lamps, and took no [extra]
oil with them" (vv. 3–4). Wisdom manifested itself in watchfulness that anticipated a potential delay and the need for
additional supplies of oil (v. 13). In the end, those additional
supplies made all the difference for the wise virgins. No wonder that Christ applies the meaning of the parable as follows:

"Watch therefore, for ye know neither the day nor the hour wherein the Son of man cometh" (v. 13).

But we shouldn't imagine that Christ is simply praising a watchful character. There are people in life who are more careful and vigilant than others. But that's not what Christ is referring to. True watchfulness is a fruit and evidence of true grace. We could define it as that *grace of the Holy Spirit in the heart and life of the believer that causes him to reckon with Christ's coming.* By nature, we lack this watchfulness. We might be careful to live a successful life in this world. That could be called an earthly, unsanctified kind of watchfulness. But the unbeliever cannot and does not have grace to approach life beyond death fittingly. He sees things in an earthly light. Although he may believe in an intellectual way that Christ will one day return on the clouds, he does not see any need for spiritual watchfulness, nor does he know how to watch. But when God works His grace in our hearts and calls us out of darkness into His light, He gives us His Holy Spirit, and with this Spirit comes the grace of watchfulness.

The Savior

Christ unveils Himself in this parable in at least three ways:

1. *As the delaying bridegroom.* Elsewhere Christ presents Himself as the bridegroom of His church (e.g., Matt. 9:15; Mark 2:19). His relationship is one of covenant with His people. He is theirs, and they are His. He has gone to prepare a place for His bride (John 14:1–2). Yet He also delays His return. He does this not because He cannot be on time. Instead, He does it to test His bride and also make her long more eagerly and earnestly for His return. Ultimately, He

has His own reasons for delaying, but the bride's response should be to trust and wait for her bridegroom.

2. *As the knowing judge.* When Christ returns as bridegroom, He shows that He knows His bride. "They that were ready went in with him to the marriage" (v. 10). The wise virgins are admitted into full, lasting, and perfect communion with Him. On the other hand, He says to the foolish, "I know you not." Christ has perfect knowledge of each person, and none of those whom He does not know will enter into the marriage supper with Him.

3. *As the warning wisdom.* The five virgins who entered into the marriage with the bridegroom were said to be wise (v. 2). But the wise do not have this wisdom of themselves. They are born foolish like every other child of Adam, who in sin has forsaken God. Christ, however, the Wisdom of God, warns us in this parable not to be foolish. We need to heed Him, for He knows all things perfectly. He can furnish us with wisdom and grace so that we will not be ashamed in the last day.

The Searchlight

This parable searches us chiefly on whether we have the grace of God in our hearts that shows itself in true wisdom and watchfulness. Let us not assume we have these things. That would be a sure sign that we are foolish. Let us pray to have the following three types of watchfulness:

1. *Watchfulness against sin.* When looked at in the light of eternity, sin appears to be a very serious thing. It is crucial that believers are careful and watchful against sin. Solomon reminds us to keep our hearts diligently (Prov. 4:23). Even

after grace, we can be very misguided about our own hearts and actions. Regular self-examination is crucial. We need to see where sin has found inroads into our lives, where coldness has set in, where unbelief has found a foothold. We need to confess sin and seek to mortify it through the Spirit's grace.

2. *Watchfulness through the means of grace.* The means of grace strengthen and support a watchful spirit. The primary means of grace, of course, is Scripture. God's Word not only reminds us constantly to be watchful, but it also directs us to mistrust the world and its thinking. By nurturing faith, Scripture also will take our focus from this world and fix it on the world to come. Prayer and attendance at family and public worship will help us to commune with Christ, and communion with Christ now will help prepare us for communion with Christ at His coming. May we not come to the final day and hear the words "I know you not" (v. 12). This means that we never had a true relationship with Him. Use the means of grace faithfully, praying that a true and living communion with Christ may be established and strengthened through them.

3. *Watchfulness for the Savior's coming.* Christ repeatedly stressed that His coming, though certain, would be unexpected. It would happen when people did not expect it (Luke 12:40). True Christians should stir themselves to be ready at any time, to have at all times what is needed should Christ return. Frequent reflection on Christ's beauty and heaven's happiness will help cultivate a readiness to meet Christ in the air (1 Thess. 4:17). Actively striving against worldliness and a worldly mindset expresses a watchful spirit. Praying for Christ's coming, like the bride of Revelation (22:17), will

excite such a spirit. Evangelism in our families and communities will help increase a readiness for Christ's coming.

It is not too late to be watchful. Let us confess our lack of watchfulness, our preoccupation with this world and with the things of time and sense. Let us pray for grace to live in the light of eternity. Let us pray to be made ready to meet Christ at any time. The parable is clear about the consequences of a lack of watchfulness. Those who foolishly neglect their duty to watch for Christ's coming will be unprepared to meet Him and will ultimately be sent away from the marriage supper of the Lamb.

Questions

1. Prove from the parable that the five foolish virgins do not represent people from the world, but rather professing Christians.

2. Some think they can be Christians without it affecting their lives very much. What does the fact that the foolish virgins had only a minimal amount of oil with them say about this?

3. How is the delay of Christ's coming in one way a mercy, and in another way a test of our watchfulness?

4. Why is it more difficult for those of us in relatively free and rich societies to be watchful? How should we fight against this?

5. Think of someone you know, among your family or circle of friends or whom you have read about, who you think lives a life of watchfulness. How does this watchfulness show itself in practical ways?

6. After being shut out of the wedding feast, the foolish virgins cry, "Lord, Lord, open to us" (v. 11). In answer, the bridegroom says that he does not know them. Christ had earlier warned that not everyone who says to Him, "Lord, Lord," shall enter into the kingdom of heaven. What does Matthew 7:21–27 say is needed?

The Glory of Kingdom Stewardship

THE PARABLE OF THE TALENTS
(Matthew 25:14–30)

His lord said unto him, Well done, thou good and faithful servant: thou hast been faithful over a few things, I will make thee ruler over many things: enter thou into the joy of thy lord.

—MATTHEW 25:21

21

Christ had just finished the parable of the ten virgins, in which
He stressed the need to be watchful. Next He added the parable of the talents, teaching His disciples that watchfulness is
not simply a passive waiting for His return. To that end, He
switches from the festive picture of a wedding to a picture of
stewards who have been entrusted with their master's goods.

Some have argued that this parable and the parable of the
pounds (Luke 19:11–27) should be considered the same story.
Though there are similarities between the two, there are also
differences. Especially because the timing and setting of the two
are different, it is reasonable to conclude that they are separate
parables. Christ told other similar but separate stories—think
of the parable of the great supper in Luke 14:15–24 and the
parable of the wedding feast in Matthew 22:2–14.

The Scenery

We could summarize the parable as follows: A wealthy man
prepared to travel to a far country, but before he left, he
entrusted his fortune of eight talents to three servants, dividing it up according to their abilities. To one he gave three
talents; to a second, two talents; and to a third, one talent.
Even one talent was a substantial sum of money and would
have been equal to twenty years of work for a day laborer.

The parable tells us that the first two servants traded
with their money, gaining an equivalent number of talents
in addition to the original sum. Meanwhile, the servant
who had received the one talent went out, dug a hole in the
ground, and hid his talent.

When the nobleman returned, he commended the first
two servants and declared to both, "Well done, thou good
and faithful servant: thou hast been faithful over a few
things; behold I will make thee ruler over many things: enter
thou into the joy of thy lord" (vv. 21, 23).

How differently it went with the servant with one talent.
The man tried excusing himself. But in the process, he cast
the blame at the feet of his master, accusing him of being a
harsh taskmaster (v. 24). In response, the master pulled the
veil off the man's pretenses and ordered that he be sent into
outer darkness.

The Substance

This parable does not teach that we can earn salvation by using
our talents to do good deeds. Neither does it teach that people will lose their salvation if they fail to work hard enough.
Instead, the basic message of this parable concerns stewardship of kingdom privileges, in light of Christ's second coming.

Many limit the significance of this parable because they
misunderstand the meaning of the word *talent*. In our language it means "special ability." However, talents in Christ's
time were measurements of money, and in the parable, the
word refers to all the privileges and blessings that the Lord
entrusts to those in the professing church. It certainly
involves money and abilities, but also time, godly parents,

other relationships, political freedom, gospel blessings, spiritual teaching, and so on. It does not refer to salvation itself; notice that the third servant ultimately perishes, even with the talent. Instead, it's like we read in Romans 3:2 about the Jews, that "unto them were committed the oracles of God." Likewise, Paul writes elsewhere that to the visible church "pertaineth the adoption, and the glory, and the covenants, and the giving of the law, and the service of God, and the promises" (Rom. 9:4). None of these privileges are of themselves saving, and yet the Lord gives them, that when He returns, greater glory would return to Him.

Some have stumbled over the fact that the nobleman gave the talents "to every man according to his several ability" (v. 15). They see this as suggesting that the Lord considers natural merit in man as the ground to give more to some and less to others. This opinion, however, is unfounded. In the parable, the Lord gave the talents to servants according to their ability so that none of them could excuse themselves by claiming that the Lord gave them more or less than they were able to handle.

Despite what the unprofitable servant said, his lack of gain was not the master's fault. The men who received two and five talents could just as easily have decided to hide what they had received in order not to suffer any loss. The point is that the servant with the one talent had a wrong view of his master, and along with that, a wrong view of himself and his talent. The man's heart was not in the right place, and it shows especially in his view of his master. So, too, natural man apart from the grace of God remains unproductive and unprofitable with any and all of God's gifts, and yet he somehow tries to lay the blame for this at God's feet.

The Savior

Christ spoke this parable after His triumphal entry into Jerusalem. In it, He unveiled himself in at least three ways:

1. *The ready servant of His Father.* Christ was getting ready to depart and return to His Father, who had sent Him as His great servant. While Christ was on earth, He did whatever pleased His Father. For every moment of His life, He could give a God-honoring account of all He did. To Him, His Father was no harsh taskmaster; on the contrary, He glorified His Father in everything.

2. *The one who procures joy for His people.* Christ now was going to suffer and die. He would do so "for the joy that was set before him" (Heb. 12:2). He knew of what He spoke when He said these words to the first two servants: "Enter thou into the joy of thy lord" (Matt. 25:21, 23). In fact, by His suffering and death, He was procuring the right to enter into this "joy" and purchasing the people who would enjoy entrance into that joy.

3. *The master of His people.* Christ is the lord of the passage. He furnishes those in His visible church with many "talents." He gives His Word and His Spirit. In fact, everything we have in creation and providence comes by way of Christ's hand. Moreover, He will give those who earnestly seek Him the grace, strength, and wisdom they need to trade with their talents. He will also furnish them with a proper view of Himself, of themselves, and of life. Meanwhile, He

will also send all wicked servants, who neither loved nor honored Him, into outer darkness when He returns.

The Searchlight

This parable shines a searchlight into our hearts that we might see our lives as we ought. It puts these questions to us: Do we begrudge what the Lord has given us? Do we look over our shoulders and wallow in self-pity? Do we nurture harsh views of God and what He has allotted us in our lives? To what extent do we neglect to use the privileges God has given us? Do we perhaps fail to see that we have not because we ask not (James 4:2)? What is our view of God? Do we realize there is nothing we have that we have not received (1 Cor. 4:7)?

The parable uncovers us so that we see our sinful nature. We are like the servant with one talent. We think of God as a harsh taskmaster and do not rightly own our responsibility to Him. But it also should spur us on, with God's help, to make use of our time, our resources, gospel blessings, our children and other family members, books and periodicals, the Bible and its promises, tracts, our station in life, and so on, to the salvation and edification of our own souls and of those around us. We would do well to ask ourselves this: How is our own view of God perhaps making us bury our talents? What view of God should we have instead?

Though it is certainly true that we cannot save ourselves, if we neglect the mercies that God has given, we will have no excuse when it is time for God to judge us. Let us especially look to the One who suffered and died to pay for sin and is now entered into the joy of the Lord, and await His return with eager expectation.

Questions

1. What talents have you been given? Is it true that everyone in the world has at least some part of a talent?

2. Could afflictions that God sends our way also be viewed as "talents" that we are called on to "improve" (make use of for good) through God's enabling grace?

3. Read the third servant's words in verse 24. What emotions, thoughts, and intentions were motivating this servant? What happens in our own lives when we look over our shoulder at others who have been given different responsibilities and privileges in their lives?

4. If the two other servants had put into words their view of their master, how different would their words be from the third servant's in verse 24? Put into words what they might have said.

5. Some have tried to give spiritual equivalents to the ideas of "trading" and "putting money to the exchangers." Discuss what graces the Lord is looking for from His people while they wait for His second coming.

6. The parable contrasts "the joy of the Lord" and "weeping and gnashing of teeth" in outer darkness. What do these descriptions of heaven and hell reveal about these places and those who go to each?

The Glory of Kingdom Separation

THE PARABLE OF THE SHEEP AND THE GOATS
(Matthew 25:31–46)

When the Son of man shall come in his glory, and all the holy angels with him, then shall he sit upon the throne of his glory: and before him shall be gathered all nations: and he shall separate them one from another, as a shepherd divideth his sheep from the goats.

—MATTHEW 25:31–32

22

Many of Christ's parables address the coming judgment. Matthew's gospel includes the wheat and the tares (13:24–30), the division of the fish in the net (13:47–52), and the handing over of the unjust servant to the tormenters (18:23–35). This theme of judgment returns in the twenty-fifth chapter. First, we read about the foolish virgins who are kept outside the wedding (vv. 10–12). Next is the account of the man with the one talent cast into outer darkness (v. 30). A final section deals exclusively with the subject of the separation that takes place in judgment, namely, the parable of the sheep and the goats (vv. 31–46). Strictly defined, this is a prophecy with parable-like characteristics interwoven, but we will still consider it as a parable.

The Scenery

It is important to notice the parable's context. The disciples ask in Matthew 24:3, "Tell us, when shall these things be? and what shall be the sign of thy coming, and of the end of the world?" Christ seems not to give them a specific answer to their question; He highlights not so much *when* these things will take place, but the *manner* in which they will take place. In chapter 25, He concludes the parable of the ten virgins by saying, "Watch therefore, for ye know neither the day nor the hour wherein the Son of man cometh" (v. 13). At the close of the parable of the talents, He encourages diligent use of the things God calls us to steward. Now, the parable of the sheep and goats also indicates how the end of the world will come.

It is also important to notice the parable's imagery. This parable harks back to Daniel 7:13–14, where Daniel receives a vision of the Son of Man coming with the clouds of heaven. Now, Christ speaks of Himself coming "in his glory" to sit on "the throne of his glory" (v. 31) for a universal judgment. The imagery He uses of sheep and goats raises important questions. Why these two animals? Is this a common illustration used from everyday life (cf. v. 32)? Why are the sheep on the right, and the goats on the left?

First, we can say that the term *sheep* is often reserved for the people of God throughout the whole Bible (cf. Isa. 53:6; Jer. 23:1; John 10). Sheep can lose the way, but, generally, they will listen to the voice of the shepherd. Usually, with one gesture from him, they will form a flock and follow after him. They are not dominant animals. We can readily understand why God's people are referred to as sheep in the parable.

But in Israel, many herds included both sheep and goats. Goats are known for being playful and fun. However, they are also harmful and destructive. You can often tell where a goat has been by the destruction it leaves behind. The book of Daniel uses the figure of a goat for worldly power that is a destructive force (see 8:5–8). Although sheep eat only grass, goats will try to chew on whatever they can. Goats need to be separated from sheep at the end of the day; otherwise, they will wreak havoc among the sheep during the night. They try to dominate the sheep if they can. They play tricks and try to delude. No wonder that this parable refers to the wicked as goats.

According to works of antiquity, the place on the right of the king or emperor was regarded as a place of honor, while the left was reserved for those who did not have his special favor. This explains the separation in this parable. The sheep are placed on Christ's right hand, indicating the favor with which they are viewed. The goats are placed on His left, indicating the disfavor and condemnation to which the wicked will be exposed in the great day of judgment.

It's important to note that Christ does not give us an exhaustive description of the judgment here. For example, there is no explicit mention of Christ's atoning work or the forgiveness of sins, though the gospel is implied in phrases such as "Come, ye blessed of my Father, inherit the kingdom prepared for you from the foundation of the world" (Matt. 25:34). Elsewhere in Scripture, more is told us about the judgment (e.g., Rev. 20:11–12). The focus in this depiction of the judgment is the final, just, and perfect separation that will be made between the Lord's people and those who are not His.

The Substance

Christ's coming to earth as a man and His time here on earth were part of His humiliation. But, in this parable, Christ pictures Himself coming in glory with all the holy angels. As He is seated on His glorious throne, all the nations are gathered in front of Him. Like a shepherd does at day's end, Christ divides the "flock" of humanity into two: the sheep and the goats.

The parable emphasizes separation. Throughout time, worldly people have mingled among God's true people like goats among sheep. Here, the two are finally separated. It's true that there is an initial separation when God effectually calls His sheep and saves them. That is a separation by grace. We could also say there is a separation at death, as it pertains to the intermediate state. A great gulf is fixed at death between the righteous and the wicked (Luke 16:26). But the separation in this text begins the final separation, in which the wicked and the righteous will never again be seen together. The wicked will go into everlasting darkness, while the righteous shall inherit the kingdom prepared for them from the foundation of the world (Matt. 25:46).

To His people, Christ will say "come." To hypocrites and worldlings He will say "depart." God's people are "blessed of my Father"; unbelievers are addressed as "ye cursed." God's people inherit a kingdom "prepared from the foundation of the world"; the wicked join the devil and his angels in the fire. In God's book, you are either one or the other.

The parable emphasizes communion. There are a number of ways in which this parable emphasizes communion. Notice, first, how Christ identifies Himself with His suffering people. "Inasmuch as ye have done it unto one of the least of these *my brethren*, ye have done it unto *me*" (v. 40, emphasis added). He is their elder brother, and they are part of His family. Moreover, what they do to other "family members," they are doing to Him. Clearly, the impression Christ's words give is that the world is not a hospitable place to God's children, just as it wasn't to Christ Himself. And yet, despite all that, Christ is with and in His people.

This communion also shows itself in the lives and character of Christ's people. Christ praises actions that display hearts filled with merciful kindness (vv. 35–40). The character of the righteous resembles Christ's character. Without ostentation or calculation, they show the "mind of Christ" through a heart of love that seeks to help and provide for others in God's family. How can we account for this other than by pointing to the mercy of God flowing *to* them from Christ, their head? It then flows *from* them to each other.

Finally, this communion will prove to be a lasting communion. Christ invites His people into communion with Him forever. "Come," He says (v. 34). As their elder brother, He welcomes them into the kingdom of His Father, into everlasting fellowship and joy with the Father, Himself, and the Holy Spirit, together with the whole redeemed family of God.

The parable emphasizes condemnation. Christ's response to the goats seals their condemnation. First, we note that their lives condemn them; they reveal an absence of communion with the Savior. "Ye gave me no meat.... Ye gave me no drink.... Ye took me not in.... Ye clothed me not.... Ye visited me not" (vv. 42–44). Christ sums up how their lives were entirely graceless. The repeated use of the word *not* reveals that their lives were spent rejecting the Savior.

Second, their speech condemns them before the Lord: "When saw we thee an hungred...athirst...a stranger... naked...sick...in prison?" (v. 44). This shows that they were entirely blind to the Lord Jesus Christ and His calls. It is interesting to notice that the righteous also question the Lord's assessment of their actions. But this only shows how their hearts had been captivated by the Lord. Whether they fully understood it, their actions returned love to Him, even as they showed love to people around them.

Third, Christ Himself condemns them to eternal destruction in hell. "Depart," He says (v. 41). All their lives, they had told the Lord to depart from them. Now He sends them away from whatever enjoyments they may have had on earth, into the awful and endless pain, misery, and punishment of hell.

The Savior

Christ reveals Himself in two particular relationships in this parable. First, Christ is the king and judge over all the nations. It is worth meditating for a moment on Christ's office as judge. Proverbs 20:8 says, "A king that sitteth in the throne of judgment scattereth away all evil with his eyes." The one whom people like to think of as "meek and lowly" is also a great and glorious king who has ascended His majestic throne and will sit in judgment over the nations. One look from this Christ will be enough to cause all the unrighteous to be vanquished, whether they have masqueraded as sheep or not. He executes justice and judgment.

Second, Christ is the head, brother, and vindicator of His people. What a magnificent thought that Christ, who exercises the right of judge, is not content to portray Himself simply as a distant sovereign, but is bound to His people as their head and brother! If Joseph did not hide his affection for his brothers in the court of judgment (Gen. 45:1–15), Christ's love for His people will be infinitely more radiant. More specifically, Christ's use of the term "brethren" (v. 40) reminds us that He was made like His brethren, and He is not ashamed to call His people His brethren (Heb. 2:11–12). He became like us that we might be made like *Him*. Christ's identification with His brethren highlights the deep significance of His mediatorial office. Because He took His brethren's condemnation on the cross, He can also vindicate them before the entire world and induct them into the eternal inheritance of His Father. He was made the sacrificial sheep, slaughtered for the sins of His brethren, that they might share in His glory forever, with Him as their shepherd.

The Searchlight

The glory of Christ as it is shown in this parable searches us in several ways:

1. *It searches our lives.* The day that Christ will judge all nations, without exception, has been appointed. Each man, woman, boy, or girl who has ever existed has a scheduled day in court—one day for everyone. God is the judge, and this will be the final judgment. There will be no appeals. Whatever injustice has been committed against God must receive redress. Do we live in light of this?

2. *It searches our hearts.* The judgment does not draw attention to huge feats of self-sacrifice or headline-grabbing donations. It mentions the relieving of hunger and thirst and providing shelter, clothing, and visitation—small evidences of a life that is constrained by the love of Christ. We can all think of times when we have neglected the oppressed, the widowed, the poor, or the hungry.

3. *It searches our confidence.* Let no one imagine that this parable allows us to put confidence in works, even after grace. If anything, the righteous in this parable are oblivious to their works. Our hope can be only in Christ and in His work on behalf of sinners. This parable drives us outside of ourselves to the one who can give us what we need both now

and when that great day comes! How much need we have of this mediator, head, brother, and vindicator. Because of His blood, righteousness, presence, and renewing Spirit, we can be prepared to meet not only our judge, but also our elder brother and friend.

Questions

1. How does Christ's second coming help us understand His first coming? What would happen to our lives if we thought as much of the second coming as we do the first?

2. As He tells this parable, Christ is about to enter into His sufferings and death (see Matt. 26:1–2). What significance does this give to this parable?

3. Look carefully at all the things this parable says about heaven and hell. Since the devil knows he is going to hell, you might think unbelievers would know it as well. Why is this not the case?

4. Many have used this parable to promote a social gospel, saying that our good works, especially for the poor and needy, will count in the judgment. What is your response?

5. What does this parable leave us to feel and do?

The Glory of Christ the King:
The Parables of John

The Glory of the King's Sacrifice

THE PARABLE OF THE SHEEPFOLD
(John 10:1–18)

I am the good shepherd: the good shepherd
giveth his life for the sheep.

—JOHN 10:11

23

This parable is often known as the parable of the good shepherd, and certainly the good shepherd is central to the parable. Yet Christ also spends a considerable amount of time speaking about Himself as the door. He also speaks at length about thieves and robbers who try to climb over the wall of the sheepfold. Calling this the parable of the sheepfold will help bring these elements together.

The Scenery

Let's look first at the parable's context. At the end of chapter 8, Christ had declared Himself not only to be greater than Abraham, but also as "I am" (see 8:58). The divine name "I AM THAT I AM" was first used in the narrative of the burning bush in Exodus 3:14. The people properly perceived that Christ's use of this name meant that He was claiming full divinity for Himself. They showed their rejection of that claim by taking up stones to stone Him. It is at this time that Christ again "hid himself, and went out of the temple, going through the midst of them, and so passed by" (8:59).

As Christ left the temple, however, He continued His ministry. He did something no mere man had ever done: He healed a man born blind (9:7). Christ not only gave the man physical sight, He also brought him to confess Christ's name and worship Him as the Son of God (9:38). In the process, the man was cast out of the synagogue (9:34; cf. v. 22).

It is in light of this that Christ gives us one of the loveliest depictions of Himself in all of Scripture. He reveals Himself with two "I am" statements, saying that He is the "door" (v. 7) and the "good shepherd" (v. 11). These two "I am" statements belong together. As shepherd, Christ owns, guides, and provides for His sheep. As door, He is the one through whom His people enter the community of His sheep and come to enjoy the benefits of belonging to the shepherd. The Old Testament background of these pictures can be found in Jeremiah 23:1–4 and Ezekiel 34. There the Lord portrays Himself as the true shepherd who re-gathers His people who have been scattered by false shepherds.

Sheepfolds in Christ's day were often fields enclosed by large walls, which were sometimes several feet high. At night, the shepherds would often bring their flocks to these enclosed areas. There was also a doorkeeper (porter), usually a hired servant from a nearby village, who would keep watch over the flock at night. The high walls and the doorkeeper (porter) helped keep the sheep safe from thieves, who would often try to break in and steal sheep. Some even say that the custom in those days was for the shepherd to lie down in the gate of the fold to prevent any person or animal from getting in or out. If this is true, it would give additional significance to the fact that Christ calls himself the door.

Moreover, Christ makes mention that the sheep hear the voice of the true shepherd. In those days, it was not uncommon for different shepherds to mix their flocks at night. When morning came, it would be their duty to separate their flock out from the mass of sheep, which usually wasn't a difficult task. Some shepherds carried pitch pipes. Their sheep's ears were tuned to a specific note or melody, and when the shepherd played it, his sheep would come to him. Shepherds would also often give their sheep names and train them to respond when they called them by those names. So the shepherd's gathering of his sheep was an easy task, and there was no worry that the sheep would get mixed up and confused. It is also important to notice that the shepherd would go before his sheep (v. 4). This was a protective position. Should the flock run into difficult terrain, robbers, or wild beasts, the shepherd would stand between his sheep and the situation in order to be able to defend his flock. This is the parable's scenery.

The Substance

John's parables, even more than those of the other gospel writers, focus heavily on Christ. For this reason, there is some overlap in the discussions of substance and the Savior in this chapter and the next. Chapter 10:1–18 can be roughly divided into three sections, and each makes a distinct point. The first section is Christ's parable proper (vv. 1–6). Here Christ introduces Himself as the *true* shepherd. This section emphasizes the contrast between Christ (the good shepherd) and the Pharisees (those who are but hirelings). Unlike the Pharisees, Christ cares for the sheep, knowing each of their names. His sheep recognize His voice. The porter also recognizes Him. This allows Christ full and free access to His sheep. On the other hand, the sheep do not recognize the voice of strangers, so they will not follow the hirelings. This is exactly what took place with the man who was healed in the previous chapter.

Despite pressure from the Pharisees, he could not listen to or obey them, for they were no true shepherds (see 9:13–34). However, he knew the voice of the true shepherd and followed Him "out of the synagogue" and into the "pasture," where Christ leads every one of His people (see 9:35–38).

In the second section (vv. 7–10), Christ elaborates on Himself as the saving shepherd. The picture in these verses is sheep in the fold who need to be led out to find pasture. The pasture is their source of nourishment and life. Those who had come before Christ were only hirelings; they could not give the sheep what they needed. But Christ came to save His sheep and lead them into abundant life. Thus, He is the "door of the sheep" (v. 7). Through faith in Him, every true sheep passes through this door and is saved. He is the only one who can give the sheep entrance into life.

This section too is a stinging condemnation of the Pharisees. In the previous chapter, they had cast the healed man out of the synagogue, thinking thus to cut him off from the worship of God and the fellowship of Israel. However, Christ makes clear that though the healed man has been cut off from fellowship with the Pharisees, he has actually entered into fellowship with the triune God, and thus has abundant life.

Finally, in verses 11–18, Christ elaborates on Himself as the self-sacrificing shepherd. This is where He explains how He is the *good* shepherd. He is good because He laid down His life for the sheep (v. 11), sacrificing Himself for them. Though a good human shepherd may on occasion end up giving his life defending his flock, he does not willingly lay down his life as a sacrifice for the benefit of his sheep. In fact, the death of the shepherd would expose the whole flock to danger. But Christ's sacrifice for His sheep is not just a remote possibility but, in fact, a requirement. Without it there would be none of this abundant life that Christ alone can give.

There are two additional things to notice as Christ speaks. First, He refers repeatedly to His Father (vv. 15, 17). He does this in order to show that His ministry as shepherd is not simply at His own initiative and for His own ends. Rather, He is the good shepherd at the behest of His Father and in order to manifest the Father. To confirm this connection, Christ says later in the chapter, "I and my Father are one" (v. 30). The ministry of the true, saving, and self-sacrificing shepherd has been planned within the great Trinity of the Godhead.

Second, Christ speaks of the Gentiles, though few of the Jews would be thinking of them just now. This shepherd has His chosen ones from among them upon His heart. Them He also "must bring, and they shall hear my voice; and there shall be one fold" (v. 16). As Paul would later put it, Christ's cross indeed broke down the middle wall of partition, and both Jews and Gentiles would unite in the one fold of Christ (Eph. 2:14).

The Savior

We have already seen much about the Savior in this parable. Christ's self-revelation is, after all, the substance, or central message, of the parable. In this section, let's focus more directly on the two names Christ gives Himself.

First, He is His people's door, or access (v. 7). This is true in two ways. No one can access His sheep, but through Him. Every true under-shepherd comes through Him to the sheepfold. The porter—namely, the Holy Spirit—gives access only to those shepherds who come through Christ, the door. There are many who want to come over the wall. However, the true sheep of God will not follow them. Moreover, the sheep themselves will come through the door. Through Christ they will find pasture during the day, as well as safety at night (v. 9). Outside of Christ, there is no access either to the sheep or for the sheep. Many imagine that there are doors of works, law, and self-righteousness through which they can enter into the fold. But Christ alone is His people's access.

Second, He is His people's good *shepherd*. Here Christ's focus is not so much on the care of His sheep, but on the deliverance of His sheep and on the life they have through Him. We tend to associate a shepherd with the care he gives his sheep. But God's people need a shepherd who will give them life by laying down His life for them (vv. 11, 15, 17–18). Without such a sacrifice to make satisfaction, God's people are simply sheep under condemnation, reserved for slaughter. Isaiah 53 says, "All we like sheep have gone astray; we have turned everyone to his own way; and the LORD hath laid on him the iniquity of us all" (v. 6). Christ willingly laid down His life for His sheep. In His very person, there is all that is needed for His people's life. Through Him there is a remedy for sin. Through His words and call, there is life and direction. Through His mediatorship, there is fellowship with the Father.

Calvary clearly casts its shadow upon the things Christ is teaching here. The time will soon come for this shepherd to lay down His life. It is at the cross that Christ will display most eminently that He—and no one else—is both the door to life and the good shepherd who gives abundant life.

The Searchlight

This parable is comforting to those who are counted among the sheep of God, but it is frightening for those who are not His. It is comforting for the sheep because of the manifold blessings that those who belong to God receive. They have one who died in their place; they are brought out into green pastures; they are held securely in the shepherd's hands; they receive the Father's love; they are known by the good shepherd; and they will have the abundant life. All these blessings are freely given to them. But those who are not God's sheep do not have these blessings. The only portion left for them is the unmediated wrath of God, death, rejection, and being "cast out" from the people of God.

This parable of the good shepherd gives several searchlights that should cause us all to consider our relationship to the Good Shepherd:

1. *Have we entered into life through Christ, the Door?* The ancient Israelites left the land of Egypt through blood-sprinkled doorposts, symbolizing that the way out of bondage is only through the God-provided means of atonement. So, too, every true Christian will have entered into life through Christ the Door, through faith in Him and His blood-bought salvation. This is where the Christian life must begin. However, verse 9 speaks of going out and coming in. Just as the sheep had to come back in through the door each day after being out in the pasture, so we need access through Christ on a daily basis.

2. *Do we know the shepherd's voice?* We should soberly examine ourselves, whether we have heard and heeded the Savior's voice. If we have, we will not follow a stranger's voice

(v. 5). Obviously, that does not mean that Christ's sheep never go astray. The lives of David and Peter and many other true sheep prove otherwise (Ps. 119:176). Nevertheless, ultimately, the shepherd's own voice rings loud and clear to the wandering sheep, and they recognize it and humbly heed it. Do we hear His voice? Do we follow Him in obedience?

3. *Do we need this shepherd's death?* John 9 proves that Christ's sheep do not have an easy life in this world. The healed man was beset by inquisition, interrogation, derision, and expulsion. But his Savior was more important to him than anything else. When God's people go through difficult and painful times in this world, let them consider the one who willingly laid down His life in order to conquer death for them and to give them abundant life both now and in the world to come.

Questions

1. From the context, discuss why the concept of the door is so important to this parable. In other words, why doesn't Christ suffice with focusing on Himself as the good shepherd?

2. Gather all that Christ says about the false shepherds from this passage and discuss how they show themselves today. What implications are there from the fact that the true sheep do not follow them (v. 5)?

3. Find all the references to the Father in this passage. Why does Christ mention the Father so frequently in connection with His giving His life for the sheep? How does Isaiah 53:6–10 help you answer this?

4. What are some of the marks of the true sheep of Christ that this passage gives to us? Should you despair if some or all of these do not hold true for you or if you find them so sparingly present in your life?

5. Why is the question of whether we need this shepherd's death so vitally important?

The Glory of Union with the King

THE PARABLE OF THE
VINE AND ITS BRANCHES
(John 15:1–17)

I am the vine, ye are the branches: He that
abideth in me, and I in him, the same bringeth
forth much fruit: for without me ye can do
nothing.

—JOHN 15:5

~ 24 ~

We have before us a somewhat unusual parable. Other parables of Christ involve a vineyard (Matt. 20:1; 21:33); this one, however, is about a vine, its branches, and a husbandman. Moreover, Christ doesn't first tell the parable and then give the interpretation, as He does at other times. Instead, He begins with an interpretive statement about Himself ("I am the vine") and then unfolds more about who He is, using that symbol.

The Scenery
The parable of the vine is in the context of what is often referred to as the "Farewell Address of Christ" (John 14–17). Christ knew what was soon to come (see John 13:21). He knew that He would be betrayed and handed over to death. Throughout the gospel of John we hear several times that Christ's hour had not yet come (John 2:4; 7:30; 8:20). But in the farewell discourse, Christ notes that "the hour is come" (17:1). The time of His earthly ministry was coming to a close. The moment toward which all history was pointing had almost arrived.

And so, in these chapters, Christ furnishes His church with comforts, exhortations, promises, warnings, and other things to enable His people to be what they are called to be as He leaves them and returns to His Father. In chapter 15, Christ's chief instruction to His people is to abide in Him. This idea of abiding occurs ten times in verses 4–10. In order to elaborate on this concept of abiding in Him, Christ uses the picture of a vine and its branches.

In the Mediterranean world of that day, the fig tree, the olive tree, and the vine were widely planted. The vine was known to be the most difficult plant to care for. Pruning the vines was done carefully and intentionally to both protect the vine and help it to produce fruit. So this was a familiar picture for John's original readers.[1]

Moreover, we find that vines are a common picture throughout the Old and New Testaments (see Psalm 80; Isaiah 5; Jeremiah 2; Ezekiel 17). Notably, every time the Lord compares His people to a vine or vineyard in the Old Testament, it is to accuse them of fruitlessness, of failing to be what He expected them to be. Yet now, Christ makes clear how His people can and will bring forth fruit—through communion with Him, the true vine.

The Substance

The way Christ works out the parable suggests various things about fruit-bearing. First, fruit-bearing takes place as a result of the vine's vitality. Christ states the principle this way: "Without me ye can do nothing" (v. 5). God's people need to draw life and strength from Him, just like a branch would from a vine. The vine is the mainspring of every blessing and

---

1. See Craig S. Keener, *The Gospel of John: A Commentary* (Peabody, Mass.: Hendrickson, 2003), 2:988–89, 994–96.

fruit in the lives of God's people. They are not vines themselves or branches of some institution or organization. They belong to Christ, as branches do to the vine. He is the only true, or genuine, vine. Certain people or entities might be known as vines or resemble vines, but they are ultimately not worthy of the name *vine*.

Second, fruit-bearing is the work of the triune God. Christ explicitly points to the Father here: "My Father is the husbandman" (15:1). The Father oversees all fruit-bearing. He ensures that it takes place and is glorified by it (see 15:8). And although the Spirit isn't mentioned directly in this passage, from the surrounding chapters it is clear that He is sent by both the Father and the Son to work grace in believers (14:17; 15:26; 16:13). This grace evidences itself in fruit-bearing.

Third, fruit-bearing takes place through abiding in Christ. Abiding in Christ means that there is a living connection or relationship between Christ and His people. Through this relationship, vitality flows from Him to His people. The very idea that spiritually dead sinners can be put into vital union with Christ is a great mystery! Clearly, a plan of salvation such as this could only have originated within the Godhead.

In verses 7–9, Christ expands on what it means to abide in Him. He is not simply referring to some static connection that needs to be maintained. That would not fit the picture of a vine and branches. Between a vine and its branches is a constant flow of sap. What flows from Christ to His people? Christ mentions His commandments and other words, which build a connection from His side to His people (vv. 7, 9). What then flows from Christ's people back to Him? Christ speaks here of prayers ("ye shall ask what ye will" [v. 7]). In short, the connection between Christ and His people is maintained by words from Him to them, and prayers from them to Him.

Abiding in Christ also involves His people receiving love from Him, then showing it forth to others in accordance with His commandments (vv. 9–13). The love He is speaking of is a self-sacrificing love (v. 13). This reminds us that just as the vine is not there for its own sake, so certainly neither are the branches. The vine bestows its energies and vitality on the branches, and the branches in turn receive this vitality for the sake of fruit-bearing.

Fourth, fruit-bearing is increased through pruning. Grape farmers attest to the fact that a wild-growing vine will at best produce small and sparse clusters of grapes. A grape-rich harvest depends greatly on the skill of the pruner. The pruner is not concerned about the "comfort" of the vine, but about the abundance of the harvest. He aims his cutting tool at dead wood and diseased sections of the vine, but also at healthy branches and beautiful foliage. The branches naturally tend to use the vine's sap to grow an ostentatious, bushy canopy. The farmer, however, is most concerned about fruit. As much of the vine's energy as possible must be channeled into fruit production. So he cuts back as much as is necessary to produce the greatest harvest over the longest period of time. As Christ says, "Herein is my Father glorified, that ye bear much fruit" (v. 8).

Fifth, the absence of fruit-bearing results in removal from the vine. Christ says, "Every branch in me that beareth not fruit he taketh away" (v. 2). Christ is not teaching that believers can lose their salvation. But it is possible that someone can be *seemingly* or *externally* united to Christ, but not *savingly* or *genuinely* united to Christ. The absence of fruit on such a branch proves that the vitality of Christ is not present in it. God, the husbandman, perfectly discerns this and sunders even the external connection with Christ, casting such a nominal Christian into hell. Christ explains it this way: "If a man abide not in me, he is cast forth as a branch, and is withered; and men gather them, and cast them into the fire, and they are burned" (v. 6).

The Savior

It is no surprise that we have already covered quite a bit concerning the Savior, since Christ is the very substance of this parable. After all, He reveals himself immediately with the words "I am the true vine" (v. 1). However, we need to consider two more aspects of this parable that show us something about our Savior:

1. *Christ purifies His people through His Word.* "Now ye are clean through the word which I have spoken unto you" (v. 3). Matthew Henry finds here an allusion to the Levitical law that when the Israelites entered Canaan, they were to consider the fruit of the first three years unclean (Lev. 19:23–24). In other words, a vine would be considered ceremonially unclean if it was still a "Canaanite" vine. Three years had now passed since the Lord had called these disciples and instructed them by His word. The implication here is that they have been purified by that instruction. Christ's word still remains the agent whereby He purifies His people and makes them clean (Eph. 5:26).

2. *Christ mediates between His Father and His people.* He speaks of this especially in verses 9–17. Remember, Christ said that His Father is the husbandman (v. 1). As the vine, Christ stands between the husbandman and His people, the branches. As His Father loved Him, He has loved them (v. 9). He has kept His Father's commandments and abides in His Father's love; His people ought to keep His commandments and abide in His love (v. 10). The things He has heard of His Father, He has made known to His people (v. 15). And whatever His people ask the Father in His name will be given them (v. 17). So Christ mediates between His Father and His people.

The Searchlight

This parable of Christ is as convicting as it is enlightening. Christ's words are both compassionate and soul searching. One cannot help but read this passage and be convicted by its many applications.

Do we trace all good back to the strength and life of Christ, the vine? Have we come to realize, experimentally, that without Him we can do nothing?

Also, have we been truly united to Christ, and not just formally? Does our union with Christ extend beyond just an external connection, a church membership, an outward keeping up of appearances? Have we given up on all "untrue" vines, and are we clinging by faith to the only *true* vine? What does the husbandman see when He looks at the branch of our life?

Do we submit to the pruning knife of the Lord in our life? Or are we too invested in our sense of comfort? Do we prefer leaves that soak up the sun rather than God-glorifying fruit?

Finally, if we are truly Christ's, do we abide in Him, in His *Word*, and in His love? Communion with Christ is a reality, but also a calling. Do we exercise an abiding dependency upon Christ, His Word, and His love? Does our heart go after Him in prayer in order to receive from Him in provision?

Questions

1. Whenever Christ speaks about Himself, as He does in this parable, He always seems to include the Father in His discussion. Why do you think He does that?

2. Christ doesn't speak in this parable about being grafted into Him as we find it elsewhere (e.g., Romans 11). Yet it is clear that not every branch is in Christ the same way. Explain the significance of this truth.

3. What binds Christ and believers together (see especially John 15:7–12)?

4. Does the picture of the vine and its branches also carry over in terms of the seasons in the life of the Christian—spring, summer, fall, winter? Explain your answer.

5. Explain verse 11 in terms of the picture of the vine and the branches. What is this joy of which Christ is speaking?

Conclusion

Full Glory

NO MORE IN PARABLES
(John 16:12–33)

When he, the Spirit of truth, is come, he will
guide you into all truth: for he shall not speak of
himself; but whatsoever he shall hear, that shall
he speak: and he will shew you things to come.
—JOHN 16:13

Perhaps you don't remember much about the day when you stopped learning the letters of the alphabet and started reading words. But you may have seen children make this transition. Individual letters become parts of a bigger reality, a word. This example might help us to understand the transition Christ speaks to His disciples about in John 16.

Christ had used many parables to teach His disciples. But on the night He was betrayed, as He was about to go to the cross, He told them that the days of parable-teaching would be a thing of the past. He said, "These things have I spoken unto you in proverbs [literally, *parables*]: but the time cometh, when I shall no more speak unto you in proverbs [parables], but I shall shew you plainly of the Father" (John 16:25). These are remarkable words. Christ is basically saying, "Parables were good to begin with, but I won't leave you with only the elementary things. I will take you to the next step. Instead of *parables*, I will use *plainness*."

Christ was here referring to the ministry of the Holy Spirit in their lives. He had just announced that "when he, the Spirit of truth, is come, he will guide you into all truth: for he shall not speak of himself; but whatsoever he shall hear, that shall he speak: and he will shew you things to come" (John 16:13). John Calvin says about this verse, "The disciples were far above those who had no relish for the word of the Gospel, and yet they were still like children learning the alphabet, in comparison of the new wisdom which was bestowed on them by the Holy Spirit."[1]

Maybe you remember your teacher in one of the early grades of school telling you just a little bit about the subjects that you would study in higher grades. You may have been struggling with simple arithmetic, and your teacher might have said, "Someday you might use these numbers in formulas that help scientists send rockets into space." Your brain could not even begin to understand how arithmetic could ever get you to that point. How puzzling and overwhelming your teacher's words would have been! That is something of what the disciples must have felt when Christ told them that He would no longer teach them in parables on the night before His death.

A Gradual Dawning

Imagine that the changes from night to day and from day to night were sudden, instead of gradual. Heavy darkness would give way suddenly to broad daylight and broad daylight to heavy darkness. Sudden transitions like that would leave us reeling, wouldn't they? We admire the Creator's wisdom in designing a gradual dawning of the day, when light begins faintly on the horizon, painting hues of orange and pink, while the blackness of night slowly recedes. Even when the morning light has arrived, it still takes some hours before the strength of the noonday sun hits us.

---

1. John Calvin, *Commentary on the Gospel According to John*, trans. William Pringle (Grand Rapids: Baker, 1957), 2:155.

The parables of Christ were part of the gradual dawning preparing for the full light of Calvary. Remember, it was just before He went to the cross that Christ spoke of the transition away from parables. This is an important point. The parables had been leading up to Calvary—introducing the disciples slowly but surely to the mysteries of what would happen there. They were like the early stages of morning light, making way for the full splendor that could be seen there. The truths they taught could be plainly seen unfolding by those who believed, as Christ accomplished redemption for His people. There He paid the ultimate price for their entrance into the kingdom of God.

There are people who enjoy reading the parables more than other parts of the Scriptures. A reader of one of the four gospels may prefer these simple, seemingly harmless stories over the more disturbing narratives detailing Christ's sufferings and His death on Calvary. But a true student of the parables will find Calvary in the parables and see the parables leading to Calvary. Think of the man who invited many guests to the supper and was dishonored and spurned. Did not this rejection climax at Calvary? Or think of the prodigal's father, who went out to meet his son. Wasn't it at Calvary that Christ went out into the far country to take for Himself the death this prodigal deserved and bring the prodigal back through the power of an endless life? Think of the shepherd who gave his life for the sheep or of the heir who was thrown out of the vineyard and killed. Both of these parables almost explicitly picture the reality of Calvary.

And so the truth of Calvary underlies every parable and is key to its meaning. Calvary explains how seed sown in the earth can produce a hundredfold harvest. It explains how none of the tares will ever affect any of the good seed. It explains how God can welcome unjust stewards into His household. Calvary explains why the publican could go to his home justified and why the persistent widow was heard. Calvary explains why the owner of the vineyard went out and took people standing idle in the marketplaces and brought them into fellowship with himself and into the inheritance of his grace. Calvary explains why the Lord can forgive debtors who owe an impossibly large debt and who should be imprisoned until they pay all that they owe. Calvary explains how the Son, rejected and despised, could become the head of the corner.

It's no wonder that Paul called the cross itself a mystery. He writes to the Corinthians, "But we speak the wisdom of God in a mystery, even the hidden wisdom, which God ordained before the world unto our glory: which none of the princes of this world knew: for had they known it, they would not have crucified the Lord of glory" (1 Cor. 2:7–8). To the natural eye, the cross couldn't possibly contain any glory—it is far too base and shameful for that. But it was not too base or shameful for Christ. In fact, it is the thing in which the most glory was hid in the most shame. And thus, Paul explains, the cross is "to them that perish foolishness" (1 Cor. 1:18). People turn away from the cross because they don't see any possible significance in it and are instead offended by it and stumble at it.

Full Clarity

In John 16:25 Christ promised a coming day of full clarity for His disciples. He wasn't speaking of heaven. Of course, knowledge in heaven will also be perfect. Instead, as mentioned earlier, Christ was speaking of the coming of the Spirit. The parables would be finished; plainness would follow. After all, the Holy Spirit works faith, sustains faith, gives clarity through faith, and steadies faith upon its object.

Imagine yourself in a vehement storm on a boisterous sea in a little boat. Somewhere in the distance is the light of a lighthouse, but between the waves, the wind, and your own fears, you can't see much of the light. But now imagine that you also had a telescope that was permanently focused on the light and was suspended in front of your eye. Your view of the light would be amazingly constant and clear. This kind of clarity is what the Lord was promising that His disciples would experience upon the gift of the Spirit.

In fact, right after Christ announces to His disciples that that time of plainness will come, He gives them a taste of it right then and there. Among other things, He says, "I came forth from the Father, and am come into the world: again, I leave the world, and go to the Father" (John 16:28). This is plain yet doctrinal teaching regarding His relationship with His Father, His incarnation, and His ascension. There is a sublime clarity to these statements! He is not using the stuff of stories, but simple and direct truth. The disciples themselves exclaim, "Lo, now speakest thou plainly, and speakest no proverb" (John 16:29).

This "gradual dawning" and "plainness" continued after Christ's death, resurrection, and ascension into heaven. Think of the clarity and directness that Peter uses on the day of Pentecost, as he says, "Him, being delivered by the determinate counsel and foreknowledge of God, ye have taken, and by wicked hands have crucified and slain: whom God hath raised up" (Acts 2:23–24). Or think of Paul's frank explanation of our total depravity and our lost state before God in Romans 3. He does not paint the picture of a prodigal son who has left his Father's house and is now wallowing in the mire. Instead, he states, "They are all gone out of the way, they are together become unprofitable; there is none that doeth good, no, not one" (v. 12). Everyone can sense the directness of such speech—a directness like that of the noonday sun!

Conclusion

As we close our study of a number of the parables, I want to ask whether you have truly understood the meaning of the parables. This is the question that Christ asked His disciples once, after a long day of speaking in parables. We read in Matthew 13:51, "Jesus saith unto them, Have ye understood all these things?" How important it is that we ask ourselves the same question!

It is possible to read and study these parables, and even find them attractive and inspiring, without being truly impacted by the truths of them. It is possible to read the words and yet never have the glory of them render you small and contrite before the One who is speaking the parables. How we need the Spirit of God and the full clarity that He provides! It is His work to guide believers into all truth.

If we truly know the ministry of this Spirit, there will be a continual conversion in our hearts and lives. We will need this as long as we live here on earth. Whether by parable, or plain doctrinal teaching, we need to be continually mastered by the message of the kingdom and the glory of the King Himself.

Those who are mastered by this unveiled glory now will themselves reign in glory with Christ in eternity (Rom. 5:17).

Questions

1. We are often rather slow or unwilling to grow in knowledge. For that reason, Peter exhorted the early Christians: "Grow in grace, and in the knowledge of our Lord and Savior Jesus Christ" (2 Peter 3:18). How can we grow, and what sorts of things should we do now that we have studied the parables?

2. In their writings, the apostles did not use parables like Christ did. Nevertheless, through the inspiration of the Spirit, they recorded and preserved the parables. What is their value today now that we have all the Scriptures?

3. We live in times when people have low tolerance for study of and preaching on doctrine. Why is this, and how do Christ's words in this passage shed light on this?

4. In what way can you say that all the parables lead to Calvary, and Calvary ultimately unlocks the meaning of them all?

5. Read 1 John 3:2b. Think of what it will be to see the Son face to face in glory and the change that will come upon believers then. How should seeing Christ in the parables now by faith bring about change? Give an example of this in your own life or in the life of someone you know or have read about.